D0146968

A New Approach to Keyboard Harmony

Also available from Norton:

A New Approach to Sight Singing, Revised,
by Sol Berkowitz, Gabriel Fontrier, and Leo Kraft

A New Approach to Ear Training,
by Leo Kraft

A New Approach to
Keyboard Harmony

Allen Brings, Charles Burkhart,
Roger Kamien, Leo Kraft,
and Drora Pershing

Queens College of the City University of New York

Edited by Leo Kraft

W • W • Norton and Company • Inc • New York

Grateful acknowledgment is made for permission to reprint the following:

Bartók, "Ballad" from FOR CHILDREN
Revised version
Copyright 1946 by Boosey & Hawkes, Inc. Renewed 1973.
Reprinted by permission

"Imitation and Inversion" from MIKROKOSMOS
Copyright 1940 by Hawkes & Son (London) Ltd. Renewed 1967.
Reprinted by permission of Boosey & Hawkes, Inc.

Britten, SERENADE
Copyright 1944 by Hawkes & Son (London) Ltd. Renewed 1971.
Reprinted by permission of Boosey & Hawkes, Inc.

Copland, APPALACHIAN SPRING
Copyright 1945 by Aaron Copland. Renewed 1972.
Reprinted by permission of Aaron Copland, Copyright Owner,
and Boosey & Hawkes, Inc., Sole Publishers and Licensees.

Stravinsky, LE SACRE DU PRINTEMPS (The Rite of Spring)
Copyright 1921 by Edition Russe de Musique.
Copyright assigned 1947 to Boosey & Hawkes, Inc.
Reprinted by permission.

SYMPHONY OF PSALMS
Copyright 1931 by Edition Russe de Musique. Renewed 1952.
Copyright and Renewal assigned to Boosey & Hawkes, Inc.
Revised version Copyright 1952 by Boosey & Hawkes, Inc.
Reprinted by permission.

Copyright © 1979 by W. W. Norton & Company, Inc.
Published simultaneously in Canada by George J. McLeod Limited,
Toronto. Printed in the United States of America.

All Rights Reserved

First Edition

Library of Congress Cataloging in Publication Data

Main entry under title:

A new approach to keyboard harmony.

1. Harmony, Keyboard.   I. Brings, Allen.
II. Kraft, Leo.
MT224.N52   786.3   78–13646
ISBN 0–393–95001–8

1 2 3 4 5 6 7 8 9 0

Contents

Introduction

A New Approach to Keyboard Harmony grew out of a body of exercises developed over many years by members of the music faculty of Queens College. Our desire for a substantial body of graded keyboard material led us to write drills of several different types. In order to meet our students' needs we created exercises based on chord progressions, sequences, and modulations; we included work in realizing figured and unfigured basses; we introduced score reading, invented special exercises in chromaticism, and added illustrations of many musical procedures from the literature of tonal music. In time, we found it advisable to add simpler, introductory exercises in order to help those students whose keyboard background was not at the college level. The present book is the result of that pedagogical experience, refined and augmented for publication.

While the importance of applying theoretical concepts at the keyboard is apparent to the teacher, it may not always be so to the student. In particular, a young musician who is not a pianist may be under the misapprehension that the theory teacher is trying to make a pianist out of every student. It is important to point out that the true purpose of studying keyboard harmony is to train the mind and the ear, not the fingers. The purposes of keyboard harmony study are twofold: one, to help the student learn to think at the keyboard; and two, to use the keyboard to learn to hear music in more than one part.

For nonpianists, the second point is crucial. A student whose basic musical experiences lies in playing a melody instrument or in singing must realize that he or she has little chance of mastering music in more than one part unless keyboard skills are developed quickly and efficiently. For example, it is likely that few flute players can imagine the sound of a four-part chorale in their minds, but we think that all can play it on the piano and thus learn to internalize the simultaneous sounds.

There is no single type of exercise that, used by itself, will fully develop the level of facility that is our goal. We have achieved the best results with a variety of exercises, approaching the materials of tonal music from different angles. Thus all of the topics indicated above are taken up in depth in this book. Not only does this make for educational effectiveness, it also offers variety in classroom experiences.

Although it is not realistic to expect each student to perform each exercise in the book, each student should do at least some exercises of each type. For this reason, every chapter includes material which makes minimal demands on the nonpianist. Within each chapter, of course, exercises are graded.

Although there is no fixed sequence to the chapters, all students would do well to begin with Chapter One. The various types of exercises may then be studied in the order that seems best suited to a particular class. We have found that all students will not benefit equally from a given exercise. The instructor should use this book in a flexible way, assigning work on the basis of the individual student's growth in musicianship at the keyboard.

Transposition is an excellent way to develop the ear and tonal memory. The exercises of the first three chapters should be played in as many keys as possible. Other exercises may be transposed as desired. The short anthology of piano pieces that comprises Chapter Eleven should be memorized, then transposed.

Special attention ought to be given to the first chapter, intended for those with little keyboard background. Such students must be prepared to spend as much time as necessary to master the simple skills presented. When they do so, they will have a firm basis for future progress. Students who already have keyboard proficiency may use this chapter to review basic material and to make sure that no basic skills have been overlooked.

To succeed in the important branch of musicianship known as keyboard harmony, a student who is not a pianist should, ideally, take at least one year of piano lessons before studying keyboard harmony and continue those lessons as long as the theory course continues. This will not only make it possible to attain a minimum level of keyboard proficiency, but will also be of invaluable help in the study of harmony, counterpoint, and analysis.

ACKNOWLEDGMENTS

We are happy to acknowledge the helpful assistance of many friends and colleagues who provided material and suggestions for this book. Thanks are due to Gabriel Fontrier, Dinu Ghezzo, Joseph Goodman, Richard Holley, Leonard Horowitz, Linda Kabo, Joel Mandelbaum, Harold Oliver, Bruce Saylor, Carl Schachter, Judith Zaimont, and Menachem Zur. In addition, we would like to express our appreciation to Karl Kroeger of the Moravian Music Foundation for making available to us the chorales by John Antes.

Our acknowledgments would not be complete if we did not include our appreciation to the many generations of Queens College students who have worked with the exercises in this book and who have enabled us to learn so much from them.

The Authors

A New Approach to Keyboard Harmony

One

Introductory Exercises

This chapter is organized around basic skills which are necessary for developing competence in keyboard harmony. The exercises fall into five categories:

> Scale and interval studies
> Improvising short melodies
> Improvising in two voices
> Hearing the difference between enharmonic intervals
> Exercises using major and minor triads

Before undertaking the main body of exercises which comprise this book, prepare yourself with the following drills in scales, intervals, and triads. Nonpianists should expect to spend some time on these basic studies. The skills to be developed through these exercises are a prerequisite to the exercises of the subsequent chapters. Exercises should be transposed as a normal part of the work.

The first step is to learn to play every scale without hesitation. To do this you must have a mental picture of how each scale looks in terms of the white and black keys of the piano. Assuming that you know the key signatures thoroughly, memorize the picture of each scale at the piano. It won't do to try to figure them out from the start each time you need them.

Practice all the major and minor scales up and down one octave. All scale fingerings are given in the Appendix, page 180. Play slowly but steadily. Increase your speed just a bit each day.

A better awareness of scale structure and tonal function may be developed by practicing the exercises that follow. They are easy to play, but require considerably more musicianship than merely playing a scale.

Scale and Interval Studies

Exercise 1·1

Practice scales in 3rds, 4ths, 5ths, and 6ths. The exercises are given in C major and are to be transposed to all major keys. Play them both melodically and harmonically, as shown. As for fingering, the complete beginner may play a two-hand version of the exercise thus:

But playing it all with one hand, especially the right, is desirable. The following right-hand fingerings will work for all keys:

> For 3rds: 2–4 2–4, etc.
> For 4ths: 2–5, 2–5, etc.
> For 5ths and 6ths: Play 1–5 when the lower note is a white key, 2–5 when it is black.

Illustrations: 5ths played in succession

5ths played simultaneously

a. 3rds

b. 4ths

c. 5ths

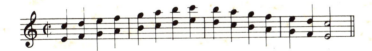

d. 6ths

Exercise 1·2

a. alternating 5ths and 6ths, ascending only

b. alternating 7ths and 6ths, descending only

c. alternating 3rds and 2nds, descending only

Exercise 1·3

Play any note as a starting point. Call that note any degree of the scale that you choose. Then complete the scale by playing stepwise from that note, either up or down, to the tonic. Play as rapidly as you can.

For example, take G as your starting note. Call it $\hat{3}$* in E♭ major. Follow it by descending ![music] or ascending ![music] to the tonic note.

Then call G $\hat{4}$. In what key is G $\hat{4}$? What notes lead down from G as $\hat{4}$ to the tonic? What notes lead up from G as $\hat{4}$ to the tonic? Play your answers.

Choose another note. Find at least five different interpretations of that note. Play each, both ascending and descending.

This exercise may be played without any written notes. If you wish, you may use the following starting points, in which key signatures are omitted. Determine the key before starting each section.

Major Keys

Minor Keys   (Use melodic minor only.)

*A carat ˆ over a number denotes scale degree.

More challenging: Play each section of the exercise above in 3rds as in *Exercise 1·1*. The first one would then go thus:

Improvising Short Melodies

Exercise 1·4

This exercise is a continuation of the previous one. Select any note on the piano. The exercise is illustrated with G as the starting note. Call G Î in G major. Invent a short melody beginning on Î and cadencing (ending) on Î. Keep the melody simple. Now take the same note and call it 2̂ in F major. Again starting on G, make up a short tune in F major that ends with a cadence on Î.

Repeat the process with G as 3̂ of E♭ major. Continue through at least five different major keys. Then do the exercise in at least five minor keys. With each melody, the tonal function of G changes, and the task of moving to the tonic in a musical way is a bit different. Try to make each tune different in character. Study the examples before starting your improvisations.

Illustrations using G as initial tone
Major

Minor

5

Improvising in Two Voices

Exercise 1·5

The procedure here is the same as in *Exercise 1·4*, except that you now start on an *interval* and progress in *two* voices, note-against-note, to a cadence on an interval that expresses the tonic chord in root position.

Illustrations using F♯–A as initial interval

Improvise similar progressions from other starting points, using only consonant intervals plus the diatonic tritone 4̂–7̂ throughout, as in section g of the illustrations above. (Depending on the situation, the teacher may wish to impose particular rules of voice leading.)

Enharmonic Intervals

It is often said that enharmonic intervals sound alike. This is manifestly untrue when a given interval and its enharmonic equivalent are heard in different tonal contexts. For example, listen to the widely different effects of the C–E and the B♯–E in the following two passages:

Strauss, *Blue Danube Waltz*   Bach, Fugue No. 4 from
                                                 The Well-Tempered Clavier, I

Though these two intervals—a major 3rd and a diminished 4th—are played on the same keys of the piano, they do not sound at all alike when heard in the context of their respective tonalities, C major and C♯ minor.

Likewise, compare the major 2nd with the diminished 3rd in the following:

Anon.   Bach, *B minor Mass*, Kyrie II
                         Alla breve

The reason that such enharmonic equivalents require different spelling is that they are so different in tonal function. Thus their musical effect is not at all equivalent.

Exercise 1·6

Play at the keyboard similar melodies containing other enharmonic pairs. You may make them up or draw upon melodies you know. If necessary, transpose the melodies in order to make the intervals in question look the same on the piano keys. Before inventing a short melody or playing one that you know, identify the key in which each of the "sound-alikes" will be heard. The following list may be used:

a. Minor 3rd   Augmented 2nd

b. Major 6th   Diminished 7th

c. Minor 6th   Augmented 5th

d. Minor 7th   Augmented 6th

e. Perfect 5th   Diminished 6th

f. Major 7th   Diminished 8ve

Triads

The four types of triad are constructed in this manner:

$$\text{major triad} = \begin{Bmatrix} \text{minor 3rd} \\ \text{major 3rd} \end{Bmatrix} \text{perfect 5th}$$

$$\text{minor triad} = \begin{Bmatrix} \text{major 3rd} \\ \text{minor 3rd} \end{Bmatrix} \text{perfect 5th}$$

$$\text{augmented triad} = \begin{Bmatrix} \text{major 3rd} \\ \text{major 3rd} \end{Bmatrix} \text{augmented 5th}$$

$$\text{diminished triad} = \begin{Bmatrix} \text{minor 3rd} \\ \text{minor 3rd} \end{Bmatrix} \text{diminished 5th}$$

Observe the following nomenclature commonly associated with the components of any triad:

> The note on which the triad is built is called the *root*.
> The note a 3rd above the root is called the *third*.
> The note a 5th above the root is called the *fifth*.

Exercise 1·7

Play each of the four triad types in three different ways:

1. Choose a note and play the triad whose root is that note.
2. Using the same note, play the triad whose third is that note.
3. Using the same note, play the triad whose fifth is that note.

Illustration

Major Triad

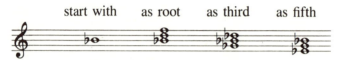

Minor Triad

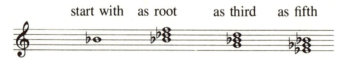

Augmented Triad

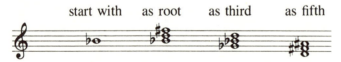

Diminished Triad

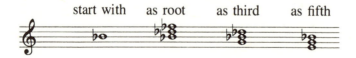

Exercise 1·8

Repeat the previous exercise, adding a fourth note with the left hand. The note to add is the root of the triad.

Exercise 1·9

Change the position of the notes in the right hand without changing the letter-names of the notes. The left hand continues to play the root of each triad.

Illustration

The change in the location of the soprano (top line) gives the name to each of these positions:

soprano has root—*position of the root*
soprano has third—*position of the third*
soprano has fifth—*position of the fifth*

Exercise 1·10

With either hand, play a triad on each successive degree of the major scale for one octave, ascending and descending, as shown below. Concentrate on learning to recognize the different sounds of major, minor, and diminished triads in the context of the scale.

Illustration

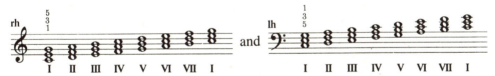

Exercise 1·11

Play a triad on each successive degree of the scale, ascending and descending. When the right hand plays, the thumb has the third, and when the left hand plays, the fifth finger has the third. This position of the triad is known as the first inversion and is identified by the figure $\frac{6}{3}$, often shortened to ^{6}.

Illustration

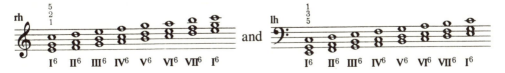

9

Exercise 1·12

Play a triad on each successive degree of the scale, ascending and descending, so that when the right hand plays, the thumb has the fifth, and when the left hand plays, the fifth finger has the fifth. This position of the triad is known as the *second inversion* and is identified by the figure $^6_4$.

Illustration

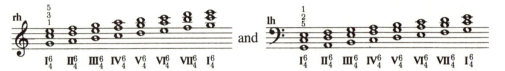

Exercise 1·13

Play a major or minor triad with the right hand. With the left hand play the corresponding scale for one octave starting with the root of the triad.

Repeat this exercise using all three soprano positions.

Play the triad with the left hand and the corresponding scale with the right hand.

Exercise 1·14

With the left hand, skip notes, as in *Exercise 1·1*. The right hand plays the triads whose roots are the notes which the left hand is playing.

Skip a 3rd

Soprano position of root   Soprano position of third   Soprano position of fifth

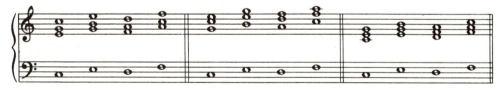

Skip a 4th

Soprano position of root   Soprano position of third   Soprano position of fifth

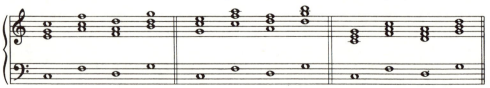

Skip a 5th

Soprano position of root   Soprano position of third Soprano position of fifth

Two

Chord Progressions

Through the practice of these exercises you will develop mastery of the chord progressions that are basic to tonal music. "Mastery of the progressions" means that you can play them fluently, without looking at the printed page, in any key.

The progressions in Chapter Two are organized in seven groups:

> Basic cadence patterns
> Expanded progressions
> More cadence chords (diatonic)
> VII and VII^7
> More cadence chords (chromatic)
> Applied (secondary) dominants and leading-tone chords
> Some Neapolitan sixth and augmented sixth progressions

Practice each progression in different ways:

> Start with the root in the soprano, then the third, then the fifth.
> Vary the register of the bass notes.
> Change the meter and improvise different note values.
> Transpose all progressions.

In the first progressions, different versions show how to vary the soprano and bass. In later exercises, do this yourself.

Basic Cadence Patterns

Exercise 2·1: I–V–I

Play each of the right-hand parts with each of the basses.

Play each of the right-hand parts with each of the basses.

Since each exercise is to be played in a definite meter, vary each exercise by playing it in a meter different from the one printed. For example, *Exercise 2·1* may be played in triple meter:

Exercise 2·2: I–V⁷–I

Combine each right-hand part with each of the basses.

Combine each right-hand part with each of the basses.

Exercise 2·3: I–IV–I

Play each of the right-hand parts with each of the basses.

Play each of the right-hand parts with each of the basses.

The progression that results from the combination of the patterns in *Exercises* *2·1*, *2·2*, and *2·3* is the single most basic of all the cadence progressions.

Exercise 2·4: I–IV–V–I

Combine each right-hand part with each bass.

Combine each right-hand part with each bass.

Without changing the bass line, II⁶ can replace IV in the cadence.

Exercise 2·5: I–II⁶–V–I

Combine each right-hand part with each bass.

Combine each right-hand part with each bass.

Exercise 2·6: I–IV–V⁷–I

Exercise 2·7: I–II⁶–V⁷–I

A cadential I_4^6 is often introduced before the V. This both delays and prepares the dominant, making the cadence all the stronger.

Exercise 2·8: I–IV–I$_4^6$–V^7–I

Exercise 2·9: I–II^6–I$_4^6$–V^7–I

Expanded Progressions

Any progression can be expanded by adding chords to the basic pattern. In *Exercise 2·10,* a I^6 is inserted after the I; in *Exercise 2·11,* VI serves the same purpose. In both cases, the interpolated chord serves to fill the bass-line jump between I and II^6.

Exercise 2·10: I–I^6–II^6–V^7–I

Exercise 2·11: I–VI–II^6–V^7–I

In *Exercise 2·12,* III links I and IV.

Exercise 2·12:   I–III–IV–V⁷–I

In *Exercise 2·13*, a neighbor chord embellishes V⁶, itself a neighbor chord.

Exercise 2·13:   I–V⁶–IV⁶–V⁶–I

In *Exercises 2·10–13*, single chords were inserted to extend the progression. In the following examples of expanded progressions, the expansion is accomplished by a group of chords which precedes and introduces the final cadential formula.

Exercise 2·14

Exercise 2·15

Exercise 2·16

Exercise 2·17

More Cadence Chords (Diatonic)

Here II_5^6 replaces II^6 in the basic cadence. Note the downward resolution of the seventh in the II_5^6, and compare with the behavior of the seventh in dominant seventh resolutions (*Exercise 2·20*). Observe that in the resolution of V^7 to I the leading tone sometimes appears to resolve down and the seventh up. In both cases the expected note of resolution is indeed heard, but in a different voice.

Invent your own additional exercises, resolving the II_5^6 to I_4^6 before the dominant.

Exercise 2·18

a.

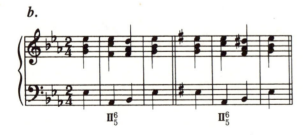

b.

c.

Exercise 2·19 illustrates three different types of $^6_4$ chords. Only two of these are new; the cadential $^6_4$ is familiar from *Exercise 2·8*.

Exercise 2·19

The next four exercises use inversions of dominant seventh chords. These abbreviations are used:

first inversion, V^6_5 appears as V^6_5

second inversion, $V^6_4_3$ appears as V^4_3

third inversion, $V^6_4_2$ appears as V^2

Exercise 2·20: Dominant Seventh Inversions

a. V^6_5

b. V^4_3

c. V^2

19

Exercise 2·21

Exercise 2·22

Exercise 2·23

VII and VII⁷

Exercise 2·24: VII in Minor

Exercise 2·25: VII⁷ in Major

Exercise 2·26: VII⁷ in Minor

More Cadence Chords (Chromatic)

Chromatically altered chords can be used in place of IV or II⁶ in a cadential progression (see *Exercises 2·6* and *2·7*).

Exercise 2·27 shows N⁶ in this role. The original cadential bass is unchanged.

Exercise 2·28 shows V⁶₅ of V replacing IV in the cadence. VII⁷ of V can be used in place of V⁶₅ of V (see *Exercise 2·29*). Note the raised fourth degree in both of these.

Exercise 2·27

Exercise 2·28

Exercise 2·29

Augmented sixth chords can also be used to precede the dominant in a cadence. Used this way, they greatly enrich the harmonic effect.

Exercise 2·30

a. "Italian" augmented sixth in cadence

b. "German" augmented sixth in cadence

c. "French" augmented sixth in cadence

Additional progressions using chromatic chords can be found under the heading "Expanded Progressions" in this chapter as well as in Chapter Eight.

Applied (Secondary) Dominants and Leading-Tone Chords

Exercise 2·31: Applied V⁷ in Major

Exercise 2·32:   Applied V⁷ in Minor

V⁷ of III   V⁷ of IV   V⁷ of V   V⁷ of VI   V⁷ of VII

Exercise 2·33:   Applied VII⁷ in Major

VII⁷ of V   VII$_{5\flat}^{6\natural}$ of II   VII⁷ of VI

Exercise 2·34:   Applied VII⁷ in Minor

VII⁷ of V   VII⁷ of IV   VII⁷ of V

Exercise 2·35

Practice the following exercise in two ways:

In each empty space play V$_3^6$ of the upcoming triad.
In each empty space play VII⁷ of the upcoming triad.

The outer voices and one of the inner voices are identical in both versions. Listen for the difference between the sound of a dominant seventh chord and a diminished seventh.

Adapted from Schumann, *Nachtstück,* Op. 23, No. 2

Some Neapolitan and Augmented Sixth Progressions

Exercise 2·36: Neapolitan Sixth

Exercise 2·37: "German" Sixth

Exercise 2·38: "German" Sixth, Inverted

Exercise 2·39: "French" Sixth, Inverted

CHAPTER

Three

Examples of Chord Usages

This chapter consists of examples of selected chord usages from the musical literature. Basic progressions are shown in a variety of styles. The exercises are in three forms:

> Piano music or piano arrangements of orchestral and choral scores
> Sing and play
> Choral music and string-quartet excerpts in open score

Practice each exercise until you can play it fluently, preferably memorizing it. Play at the correct tempo if your piano-playing ability permits. If not, play the exercises slowly, but play at a steady tempo at all times. For further practice, these exercises may be transposed.

Exercise 3·1: I–V⁷–I

Beethoven, *Symphony No. 5*, IV

Exercise 3·2: I–V⁷–I

Schubert, *Waltz*, Op. 18, No. 6

The left-hand part may be simplified and played:

25

Exercise 3·3: IV, V

Wagner, *Das Rheingold*, Scene 2

Exercise 3·4: I–IV–V⁷–I

Pachelbel, *Sarabande*

Exercise 3·5: IV, V⁷

Schumann, *Aus meinen Tränen*

Exercise 3·6: VI

Grieg, *Morning* from *Peer Gynt Suite No. 1*

I   VI   I

Exercise 3·7: V⁷–VI

Chopin, *Nocturne,* Op. 37, No. 1

V   VI

Exercise 3·8: Six Different Triads

Janequin, *Ce moys de May*

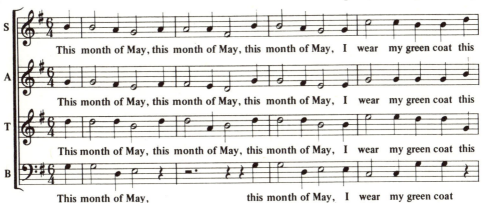

S — This month of May, this month of May, this month of May, I wear my green coat this

A — This month of May, this month of May, this month of May, I wear my green coat this

T — This month of May, this month of May, this month of May, I wear my green coat this

B — This month of May, this month of May, I wear my green coat

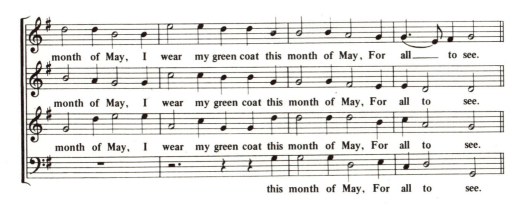

month of May, I wear my green coat this month of May, For all___ to see.

month of May, I wear my green coat this month of May, For all to see.

month of May, I wear my green coat this month of May, For all to see.

this month of May, For all to see.

Exercise 3·9: III in Minor

Ingegneri, *Response*

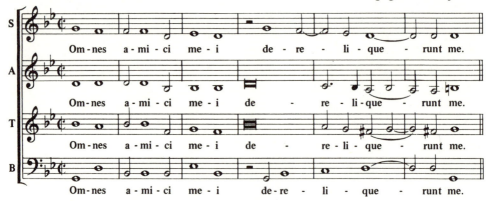

Exercise 3·10: VII in Minor

Gibbons, *O Lord, Increase My Faith*

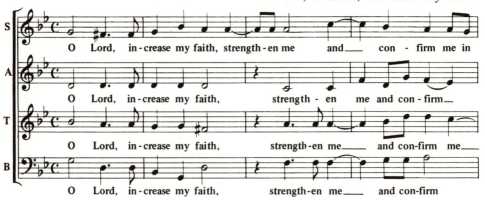

Exercise 3·11: I⁶, V⁶

Scheidt, From the *Gorlitz Organ Book*

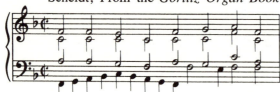

Exercise 3·12: IV⁶ in Minor

Dowland, *Lachrimae* (Simplified)

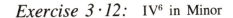

Exercise 3·13: ⁶₃ chords

Pachelbel, *Gavotte*

Exercise 3·14: II⁶

Beethoven, *Piano Sonata,* Op. 28, III

Allegro vivace

Exercise 3·15: VII⁶

Bach, Chorale Setting,
O Ewigkeit du Donnerwort

29

Exercise 3·16: I$_4^6$

Bellini, Aria from *Norma*, Act II

Won't you take these chil-dren with— you, Oh sup-port them and de - fend— them, I don't

ask for fame and hon- or, To_ your sons they_ shall be giv- en.

Exercise 3·17: I$_4^6$

Three Approaches to I$_4^6$
Mozart, *String Quartet*, K. 421, II

Exercise 3·18: I_4^6

Schubert, *Gute Nacht*

Exercise 3·19: VII[7]

Franz, *Der vielschönen Frau*

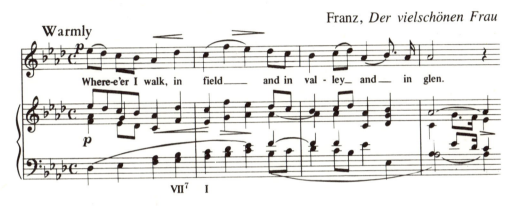

Where-e'er I walk, in field___ and in val - ley__ and__ in glen.

Exercise 3·20: VII[7] and Inversions

Gluck, Opening Chorus from *Orfeo*

Ah, in this wood__ so__ still and som - bre, Eu - ry - di - ce,

If your spi - rit, if your spi - rit can but hear us,

Exercise 3·21: V⁷ Inversions

Beethoven, *Piano Sonata*, Op. 7, II

Exercise 3·22: I–II²–V₅⁶–I

Bach, Prelude No. 1 from *The Well-Tempered Clavier*, I

Exercise 3·23: II₅⁶

Bach, Chorale Setting, *Singen wir aus Herzens Grund*

Exercise 3·24: V⁷ of IV

Chopin, *Mazurka,* Op. 41, No. 2

Exercise 3·25: V of II

Haydn, *Symphony No. 94*, I

Exercise 3·26: V⁷ of II, III

Beethoven, *Piano Sonata,* Op. 14, No. 2, II

Exercise 3·27: V of .VI

Gounod, *Faust,* Act IV

Glo - ry and hon-or to men of old —— Let us be

VI

Exercise 3·28: V⁷ of III, V

Bizet, Chorus from *Carmen*, Act I

Exercise 3·29: VII⁷ of V

Beethoven, *Piano Sonata*, Op. 13, I

Exercise 3·30:   VII⁷ of V

Brahms, *Vergebliches Ständchen*

VII⁷ of V

Exercise 3·31:   VII⁷ of V

Mendelssohn, *Song without Words*, Op. 67, No. 3

VII⁷ of V

35

Exercise 3·32: VII⁷ of II

Schubert, *Piano Sonata*, Op. 120, I

VII⁷ of II

This example contains many pianistic difficulties. Is there a simpler way to play it and still learn the chord content? Try playing all four arpeggiated notes in the left hand together, keeping them in one register; omit notes in the right hand which are doubled in the left, such as those with stems down in the first measures.

Exercise 3·33: N⁶ (♭II⁶)

Beethoven, *Piano Sonata*, Op. 27, No. 2, I

VI (V of N⁶)   N⁶

V⁷

Exercise 3·34: Neapolitan Triad (♭II)

Verdi, *Requiem,* Opening

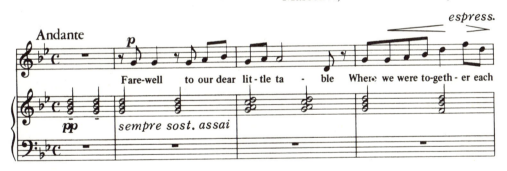

Exercise 3·35: Augmented Sixth (German)

Massenet, Aria from *Manon,* Act II

Exercise 3·36 Augmented Sixth (German)

Verdi, from *Quattro pezzi sacri*

Exercise 3·37: Augmented Sixth (French)

Verdi, *Requiem*, Opening

Exercise 3·38: Augmented Sixth (French)

Schubert, *Der Wegweiser*

Aug. 6th   V

CHAPTER
Four

Melodies to Harmonize

Harmonization of melodies at the keyboard is a practical skill required of most musicians at one time or another. For all music students it affords good practice in relating melody and harmony quickly and convincingly. Choose the chords suggested by the melody by analyzing the tune, identifying chord outlines, and determining which melody notes are chord tones and which are embellishing tones. Then improvise an accompaniment that suits the character of the melody. In performing these exercises you may accompany another student who sings or you may sing and play at the same time.

The melodies in this chapter come from many places. Many are folk songs and popular tunes. These have fairly limited chordal possibilities. Others are chosen from opera and from the art-song repertoire, and may require richer chord vocabularies.

No tempo markings are given for the folk and popular melodies. It is up to you to find an appropriate speed of performance. Often there is no ''correct'' tempo for a melody, but rather a range within which a number of speeds may be suitable. Think about the tempo of each melody, and make choices with which you feel comfortable. Try performing at least some melodies in more than one tempo, and compare the results.

Choose an accompaniment pattern that is in character with the melody. Simple accompaniment figures are often quite adequate, but more elaborate ones can lend richness and color to a melody. Following are four possible ways of accompanying the opening of Melody 1, using different chord choices and different accompaniment figures:

a.

Tell me the tales that to me were so dear, Long, long a-go, Long, long a-go;

b.

The advantages of using inversions of triads are illustrated in two versions of No. 25, *Aura Lee,* the first employing only root positions, the second including first-inversion triads:

Melodies which move predominantly by step but which are also in moderate tempos readily lend themselves to harmonizations in which both melody and accompaniment are played together. Using the style of keyboard playing already discussed in Chapter Two, in which the left hand plays only the bass while the right hand plays the three upper parts including the melody being accompanied, melody No. 3, *Go Tell Aunt Rhody,* might be harmonized as follows:

Melodies such as No. 30, *America,* are particularly suited to this style of harmonization. Continue playing *America* in the following manner:

If playing melody and accompaniment together requires considerable understanding of chord usage, playing little more than the melody in the right hand and all of the accompaniment in the left may demand greater keyboard technique. Below are two versions of No. 15, *Auld Lang Syne,* the first designed for keyboard players, the second for non-keyboard players:

The presentation of each melody in a particular key must not discourage its performance in many other keys. Indeed, if the purpose of a harmonization is to accompany the singing of a melody, the choice of key should be determined only by the vocal range of the singer, not by the ability of the pianist.

The first ten melodies may be harmonized using only two chords in each, I and either V or V^7. To be sure, even those simple tunes will gain from the use of inversions and from the addition of other chords as well.

Exercise 4·1

Thomas Haynes Bayly, *Long, Long Ago*

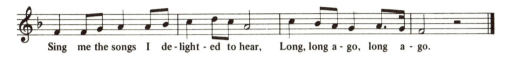

Tell me the tales that to me were so dear, Long, long a-go, Long, long a-go;

Sing me the songs I de-light-ed to hear, Long, long a-go, long a-go.

Exercise 4·2

Verdi, *Il trovatore*, Act IV

Home to our moun-tains, you shall yet take me, No fear or sor-row there shall o'er-take you.

Exercise 4·3

Traditional, *Go Tell Aunt Rhody*

Go tell Aunt Rho-dy, Go tell Aunt Rho-dy, Go tell Aunt Rho-dy the

old gray goose is dead.

Exercise 4·4

Verdi, *Rigoletto*, Act I

Allegro moderato

Dear-est name that taught my heart all the joy of ten-der

love How you wak-en sweet de-sire for the one whom I a-dore!

Exercise 4·5

Schubert, *Wiegenlied*, Op. 98, No. 2

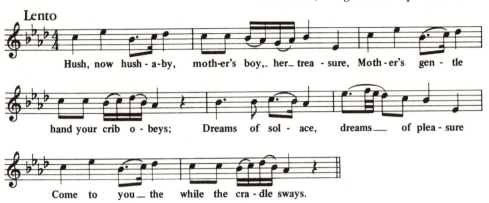

Hush, now hush - a - by, moth-er's boy, her trea - sure, Moth - er's gen - tle
hand your crib o - beys; Dreams of sol - ace, dreams of plea - sure
Come to you the while the cra - dle sways.

Exercise 4·6

Traditional, *Liza Jane*

When I go a - rid - in' I take a rail - road train; But
when I go a - court - in' I take sweet Li - za Jane.

Exercise 4·7

Mozart, *Symphony No. 39,* K. 543, III

Allegretto

Exercise 4·8

Traditional German, *O Christmas Tree*

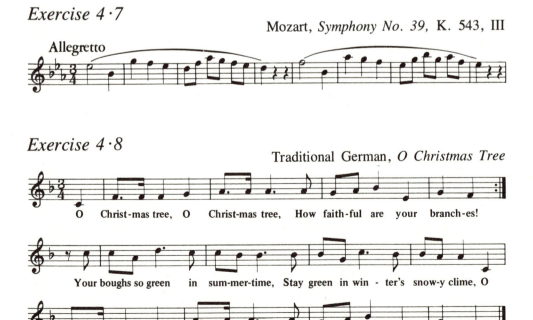

O Christ-mas tree, O Christ-mas tree, How faith-ful are your branch-es!
Your boughs so green in sum-mer-time, Stay green in win - ter's snow-y clime, O
Christ - mas tree, O Christ - mas tree, How faith - ful are your branch - es!

Exercise 4·9   Spiritual, *Joshua Fit the Battle of Jericho*

Josh-ua fit the bat-tle of— Je-ri-cho,   Je-ri-cho,   Je-ri-cho;——

Josh-ua fit the bat-tle of— Je-ri-cho,   and the walls came tum-blin' down.

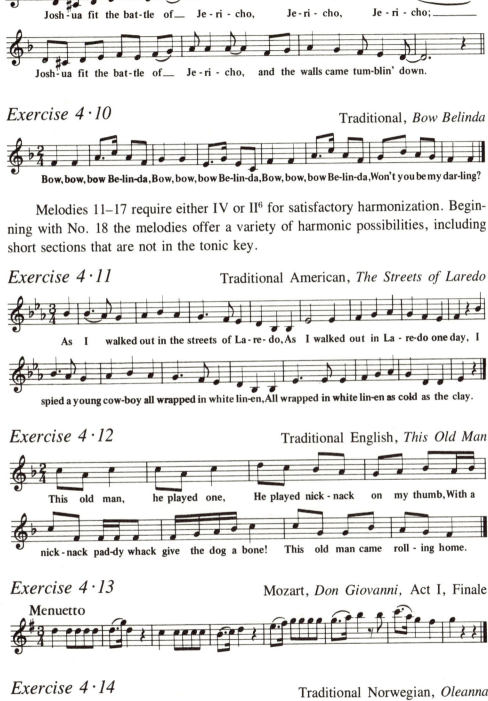

Exercise 4·10   Traditional, *Bow Belinda*

Bow, bow, bow Be-lin-da, Bow, bow, bow Be-lin-da, Bow, bow, bow Be-lin-da, Won't you be my dar-ling?

Melodies 11–17 require either IV or II⁶ for satisfactory harmonization. Beginning with No. 18 the melodies offer a variety of harmonic possibilities, including short sections that are not in the tonic key.

Exercise 4·11   Traditional American, *The Streets of Laredo*

As   I   walked out in the streets of La-re-do, As   I walked out in La-re-do one day, I

spied a young cow-boy all wrapped in white lin-en, All wrapped in white lin-en as cold as the clay.

Exercise 4·12   Traditional English, *This Old Man*

This   old   man,   he played one,   He played nick-nack   on   my thumb, With a

nick-nack pad-dy whack give the dog a bone!   This   old   man came   roll-ing home.

Exercise 4·13   Mozart, *Don Giovanni*, Act I, Finale

Menuetto

Exercise 4·14   Traditional Norwegian, *Oleanna*

O-le, O-le-an-na,   O-le, O-le-an-na,   O-le, O-le,-O-le, O-le,   O-le, O-le-an-na.

Exercise 4·15

Traditional Scottish, *Auld Lang Syne*

Should auld ac-quain-tance be for-got, And_ nev - er brought to mind? Should

auld ac-quain-tance be for-got, And_ days of auld lang syne? And

days of auld lang syne, my dear, and days of auld lang syne, We'll

take a cup o' ' kind - ness yet For_ auld___ lang___ syne.

Exercise 4·16

Franz Gruber, *Silent Night*

Si - lent night, Ho - ly night! All is calm, All is bright

Round yon Vir - gin Moth- er and Child. Ho - ly In - fant so ten - der and mild,

Sleep in heav - en-ly peace,___ Sleep_ in heav - en-ly peace.

Exercise 4·17

Traditional English, *The Muffin Man*

O do you know the Muf-fin Man, the Muf-fin Man, the Muf-fin Man, O

do you know the Muf - fin Man, that lives in Dru - ry Lane?

Exercise 4·18

Traditional, *Vive l'Amour!*

Let each jol - ly fel -low now fill up his glass, Vi - ve la com - pa - gnie!_ And

drink to the health of his beau - ti - ful lass, Vi - ve la com - pa - gnie!

Vi - ve la, vi - ve la, vi - ve l'a-mour, Vi - ve la, vi - ve la, vi - ve l'a-mour,

Vi - ve la, vi - ve la, vi - ve l'a-mour, Vi - ve la com - pa - gnie!

Exercise 4·19

Catalonian Christmas Carol

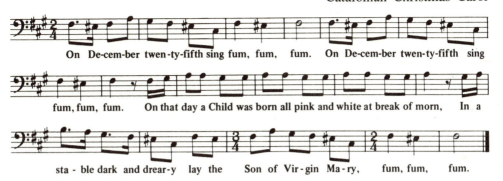

On De-cem-ber twen-ty-fifth sing fum, fum, fum. On De-cem-ber twen-ty-fifth sing fum, fum, fum. On that day a Child was born all pink and white at break of morn, In a sta-ble dark and drear-y lay the Son of Vir-gin Ma-ry, fum, fum, fum.

Exercise 4·20

Dan Emmett, *Old Dan Tucker*

I came to town the oth-er night, I heard the noise and saw the fight. The watch-man, he was run-ning 'round, said "Old Dan Tuck-er's come to town." Get out the way, old Dan Tuck-er, Get out the way, old Dan Tuck-er, Get out the way, old Dan Tuck-er, You're too late to come to sup-per.

Exercise 4·21

Traditional, *Believe Me, If All Those Endearing Young Charms*

Be-lieve me if all those en-dear-ing young charms, which I gaze on so fond-ly to-day, were to change by to-mor-row and fleet in my arms, Like fair-y gifts fad-ing a-way, Thou wouldst still be a-dored, as this mo-ment thou art, Let thy love-li-ness fade as it will, And a-round the dear ru-in, each wish of my heart, Would en-twine it-self ver-dant-ly still.

Exercise 4·22

Traditional Polish, *Krakowiak*

I come from old Cra - cow,— sure - ly you would know it, For my belt will
show it, with sev-en-ty pegs right through it. I come from old Cra-cow,— sure-ly you would
know it, for my belt will show it, with sev - en-ty pegs right through it.

Exercise 4·23

Traditional English, *Drink to Me Only with Thine Eyes*

Drink to me on - ly with thine eyes,— And I— will pledge with mine;—
Or leave a kiss with - in— the cup,— And I'll— not ask for wine. — The
thirst— that from the soul— doth rise Doth ask a drink— di - vine;—
But might I of Jove's nec - tar sup,— I would not change for thine.—

Exercise 4·24

Traditional Russian, *The Peddler*

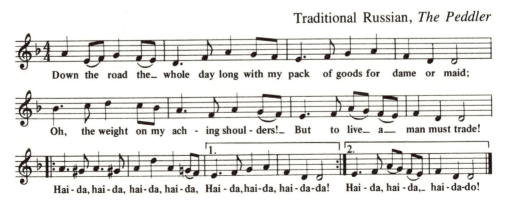

Down the road the— whole day long with my pack of goods for dame or maid;
Oh, the weight on my ach - ing shoul - ders!— But to live— a— man must trade!
1. 2.
Hai - da, hai - da, hai - da, hai - da, Hai - da, hai-da, hai - da-da! Hai - da, hai - da,— hai - da-do!

48

Exercise 4·25

Traditional, *Aura Lee*

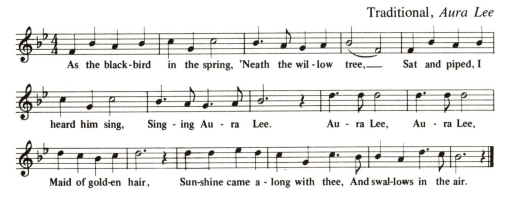

As the black-bird in the spring, 'Neath the wil-low tree,— Sat and piped, I
heard him sing, Sing-ing Au - ra Lee. Au - ra Lee, Au - ra Lee,
Maid of gold-en hair, Sun-shine came a - long with thee, And swal-lows in the air.

Exercise 4·26

Thomas Casey, *Drill, Ye Tarriers, Drill*

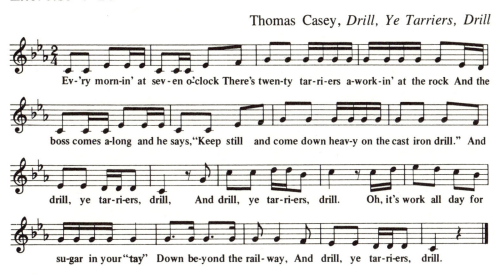

Ev-'ry morn-in' at sev-en o'clock There's twen-ty tar-ri-ers a-work-in' at the rock And the
boss comes a-long and he says, "Keep still and come down heav-y on the cast iron drill." And
drill, ye tar-ri-ers, drill, And drill, ye tar-ri-ers, drill. Oh, it's work all day for
su-gar in your "tay" Down be-yond the rail-way, And drill, ye tar-ri-ers, drill.

Exercise 4·27

Schubert, *Childhood Joy*

Moderato

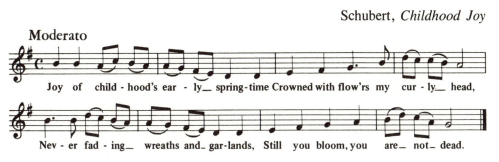

Joy of child - hood's ear - ly— spring-time Crowned with flow'rs my cur - ly— head,
Nev - er fad - ing— wreaths and— gar-lands, Still you bloom, you are— not— dead.

Exercise 4·28

H. J. Fuller, *My Bonnie*

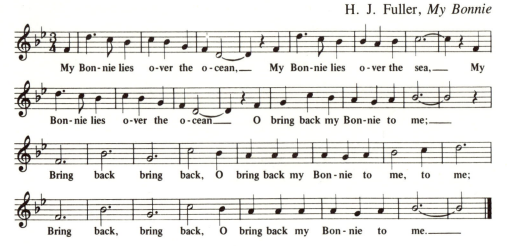

My Bon-nie lies o-ver the o-cean,— My Bon-nie lies o-ver the sea,— My
Bon-nie lies o-ver the o-cean— O bring back my Bon-nie to me;—
Bring back bring back, O bring back my Bon-nie to me, to me;
Bring back, bring back, O bring back my Bon-nie to me.—

Exercise 4·29

Verdi, *Rigoletto*, Act II

Andantino

Man-y a Sun-day morn-ing, as I was deep in pray-er
There was a fine young gen-tle-man who would ob-serve me close-ly.
Though we had nev-er ex-changed— a word, our eyes spoke. the love. that filled our hearts.

Exercise 4·30

Traditional American, *Farewell, Dear Friends*

Fare-well dear friends, I'm bound for Ca-naan, I'll tra-vel on far from this world.
Friend-ship has been my great-est plea-sure Part-ing is sad, But I must go.
I go a-way You won't be near me, Lone-ly the path when friends are far,
Yet tho' we part here on this earth, We'll meet a-gain in Ca-naan land.

50

Exercise 4·31

Traditional American, *O Bury Me Beneath the Willow*

Exercise 4·32

Traditional American, *The Erie Canal*

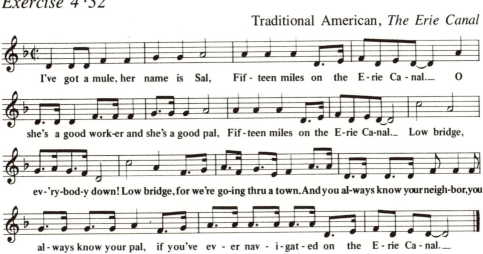

Five

Sequences

A sense of directed musical motion is produced by a *harmonic sequence,* the repetition of a chord pattern at a higher or lower pitch level. The chord pattern is usually repeated a 2nd or 3rd above or below the original. It is anywhere from a half-measure to several measures in length and may be melodically or rhythmically varied. Sequential passages may be found in themes, transitions, and development sections.

This chapter includes some of the most common harmonic sequences. Each chord progression is illustrated by an example from music literature. Progressions and musical examples should be transposed to a variety of keys.

Circle of Fifths

Exercise 5·1:   All Chords $\frac{5}{3}$

Illustrations

Handel, *Passacaille,* Variation 1

Handel, Courante from *Suite No. 14*

Exercise 5·2: Alternate Chords ⁶₃

Illustration

Mozart, *Sonata in C*, K. 545, I

Exercise 5·3: Consecutive Seventh Chords

Illustration

Mozart, *Sonata in F*, K. 332, I

A Descending Sequence in Two Versions

Exercise 5·4: Descending Scale in Soprano,
Alternating 4ths and 2nds in Bass

Illustration

Chopin, *Mazurka,* Op. 68, No. 3

54

Exercise 5·5:   Descending Scale in Bass,
Alternating Root-Position and First-Inversion Triads

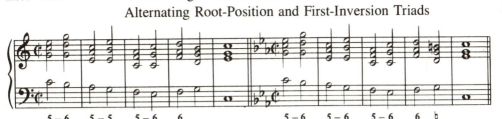

5 – 6   5 – 5   5 – 6   6   5 – 6   5 – 6   5 – 6   6   ♮

Illustration

Beethoven, *Sonata,* Op. 79, III

p dolce

Ascending Sequence

Exercise 5·6:   Ascending Scale in Soprano,
Alternating 5ths and 6ths (or 4ths and 3rds) in Bass

Illustration

Pergolesi, *La serva padrona,* Act I

Voice: No-thing but trou - ble   all day and night,_____ all day and night,

Piano

You can be sure,   to rouse my ire,   I'm all a-fire,   yes, yes, a-fire

Exercise 5·7:   Alternating 5ths and 6ths
between the Bass and an Upper Voice

Soprano   5 – 6   5 – 6   5 – 6   5 – 6
Bass

Illustration

John Dowland, *Come Again, Sweet Love*

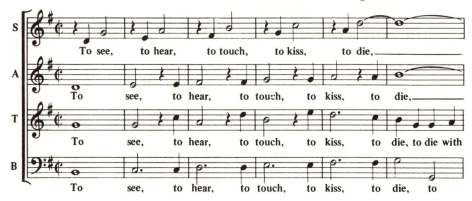

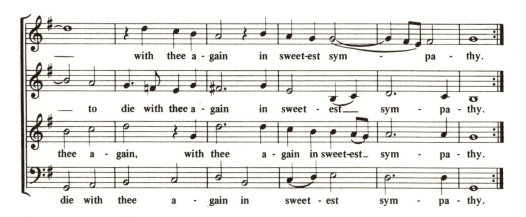

Exercise 5·8:

The Same, with Chromatic Passing Tones

Soprano   5   6   5   6   5   6
Bass

Schumann, *Piano Quintet,* I

CHAPTER
Six

Modulation

Introduction

While this book includes as little theoretical discussion as possible, a few definitions and observations will be useful before the study of this chapter.

In modulation, the relation between the original key and the new key is often spoken of in such terms as "close" or "distant" or "remote." There are many shades of difference between key relationships, but we will simply make one large distinction by grouping them all under one of two headings: *diatonic* and *chromatic*. We define a diatonic key relation as one in which the tonic triad of the new key lies within the unaltered (diatonic) scale of the original key. For example, if the original key is C major, the diatonically related keys are D minor (II in C), E minor (III in C), F major, G major, and A minor, a total of five. From C minor the possibilities also total five: E♭ major, F minor, G minor, A♭ major, and B♭ major. All other key relations exhibit some degree of chromaticism, ranging from very slight to very great. These are defined as chromatic.

The terms *diatonic* and *chromatic* may also be applied to the modulation process itself, regardless of the key relation involved. A modulation can be accomplished purely diatonically, or may admit chromaticism to a degree. One important type is the essentially diatonic modulation that is embellished by chromatic chords of some kind, as, for example on pages 21-22.

After playing or hearing certain modulations you may say, "But I still hear the original key." This does not mean that the modulation is poor. Indeed, hearing a new key in terms of the original one can even be desirable if the original is understood as the main key of a composition, and the new as only a temporary digression.

The number of ways to effect a given modulation is virtually infinite, but some pathways are taken more frequently than others. This chapter is confined to usages that lend themselves to short keyboard exercises of a type that requires the player to invent at least a small part of the modulation. Another way of studying modulation—and one highly recommended—is to select short, clear examples of modulation from the literature and transpose them. Many of the chorales given on pages 82-87, are admirably suited to this purpose.

A Preparatory Exercise

Choose one particular triad, major or minor, and progress to cadences in all keys in which that triad is a diatonic chord. For example, take a D minor triad and proceed thus:

> call it I and cadence in D minor; then
> call it II and cadence in C major;
> call it III and cadence in B♭ major;
> call it IV and cadence in A minor;
> call it VI and cadence in F major.

Here are a few models, starting with a D minor triad:

Experiment with different routes to the cadence, such as:

A Special Case

Call the given chord (D minor) V and move *diatonically* to a V♯–I cadence in G minor, for example, thus:

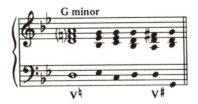

This succession avoids the chromatic half step F♮–F♯. Do not use chromatic intervals in this exercise. They will be dealt with later.

Now take a major triad and treat it similarly. It cannot be a II, of course, but it can be a VII in minor, as well as a IV♯ in minor.

59

Further Advice

The given triad may have root, third, or fifth in the soprano; practice all three possibilities. Favor smooth voice leading; in particular, use mostly stepwise motion in the soprano. A more conclusive effect is produced if the exercise ends with the tonic note in the soprano, but this is not mandatory. **Nota bene:** It is especially recommended to aim first for a chord of *sub*dominant function—some form of IV or II—and *then* to go on to V–I.

Exercise 6·1

Do the exercise starting with each of the following as the given chord:

Continue the same exercise with chords of your own choosing.

The Pivot Chord Approach
1: The Pivot Is the I Chord of the Original Key

Practice playing modulations that are conceived as in the following scheme:

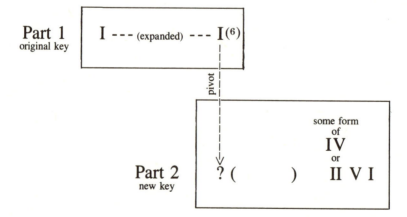

Comment on the Scheme: Part 1

Start with a major or minor triad. Consider it a I chord. Then expand (prolong) this I chord by means of a short progression that begins and ends on I (or I⁶). For example, here are four very common expansions chosen from among the hundreds of possibilities:

a. Expand the I by a neighbor-note motion $\frac{5-6-5}{3-4-3}$:

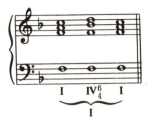

$$\text{I} \quad \text{IV}^6_4 \quad \text{I}$$
$$\underbrace{\qquad\qquad}_{\text{I}}$$

b. Expand the I by moving to I^6 through a passing V^6_4 or VII^6:

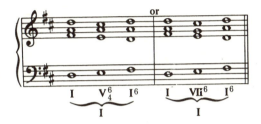

$$\text{I} \quad \text{V}^6_4 \quad \text{I}^6 \qquad \text{I} \quad \text{VII}^6 \quad \text{I}^6$$
$$\underbrace{\qquad}_{\text{I}} \qquad\qquad \underbrace{\qquad}_{\text{I}}$$

c. Expand the I using I^6 and inversions of V^7:

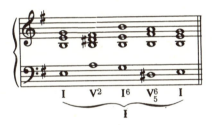

$$\text{I} \quad \text{V}^2 \quad \text{I}^6 \quad \text{V}^6_5 \quad \text{I}$$
$$\underbrace{\qquad\qquad}_{\text{I}}$$

d. Expand the I by means of the progression $\text{I–II}^4_2\text{–V}^6_5\text{–I}$
In each case, the final chord in Part 1 will be I or I^6 in the original key.

Comment on the Scheme: Part 2

The first chord in Part 2 is the last one in Part 1. Conceive of this chord as the *pivot* chord—that is, a chord *common* to both keys. The pivot is symbolized in the scheme as question mark (?) since its function will vary, depending on the key of Part 2. Now move toward a cadence in the new key. Note that the antepenultimate chord must be of *sub*dominant function; aim for this chord after playing the pivot. In some cases the pivot will itself be subdominant (as in the second of the two models given below). Part 2 can often be accomplished in just three or four chords, but more may be used if needed or desired by the player. Such additional chords are symbolized in the scheme by parentheses ( ).

There is no end to the musical invention possible within this scheme. In the following two models notice the motives indicated by the brackets.

Two Models of Diatonic Modulation

I becomes VI

G major I - - *(expanded)* - - I

B minor VI   IV   V$^6_4$ $^5_3$ I

I becomes II

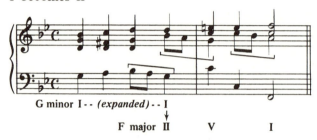

G minor I - - *(expanded)* - - I

F major II   V   I

Nota bene: In this and all subsequent exercises, it is not forbidden to strike the I or I^6 of the new key *before* the final chord is reached. Indeed, a more persuasive effect is often produced by having *two* (or more) V–I progressions in the new key. The last one will, of course, be the final cadence, and therefore in $^5_3$ position; the interior one(s) may use inverted forms of V and I. For example, the model just shown could be realized thus:

G minor I - - *(expanded)* - - I^6

F major II^6 V$^4_2$ I^6 V   I

Throughout this exercise, avoid chromatic voice leading, particularly the interval of the chromatic half step (e.g., C♮–C♯.

Exercise 6·2

Using the scheme on page 60, play ten different modulations—five starting in major and five in minor. Try starting all ten on the same tonic note, then starting each on a different tonic.

The Pivot Chord Approach
2: The Pivot Is Other Than I in the Original Key

In compositions, the pivot is often a chord other than I in the original key. To promote the discovery and use of such pivots, we will adapt our scheme as follows:

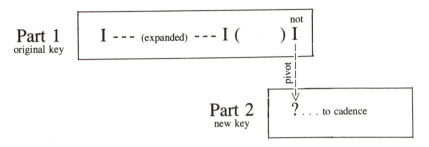

Here is one possible solution:

IV⁶ becomes II⁶

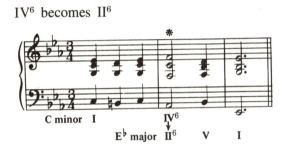

Observe that the F minor chord (see asterisk) is both 1) the pivot chord and 2) of subdominant function in the new key. Therefore, it can be followed immediately by the final cadence.

Exercise 6·3

Using this revised scheme, modulate from A major to all five diatonically related keys. Repeat, starting in a given minor key. Wherever possible, use a pivot chord that, as in the model, is of subdominant function in the new key.

The Pivot Chord Approach
3: Embellishing the Modulation with Applied (Secondary) V and VII Chords

We noted in the introduction to this chapter that a diatonic modulation can be embellished by chromatic chords. Review the nonmodulating exercises in Applied (Secondary) Dominants and Leading-Tone Chords (given on pages 22-23), which are based on the idea of a diatonic foundation chromatically embellished. Here we simply extend this idea into the realm of modulation.

Illustration

The schemes presented on pages 60 and 63 can still serve as a starting point. Let us take the model solution just presented (page 63) and embellish some of the chords in it with applied V and VII chords. Here are two possible solutions:

a. IV⁶ becomes II⁶

C minor   I

E♭ major   II⁶   V⁶₄ ₋₅₋₃   I

b. IV⁶ becomes II⁶

C minor   I   IV

E♭ major   II   V   I

Take special note that the hitherto disallowed interval of the chromatic half step now occurs in connection with the use of the applied (secondary) chords, such as the E♭–E♮ and A♭–A♮ in the illustration above.

Exercise 6·4

Play the following modulations, embellishing them with applied V and VII chords. Choose different keys and experiment with different soprano positions. Remember that the opening I is also to be expanded and that, as shown in the first solution, this expansion may also make use of applied V and VII. Observe that interior chords, including the pivot, may be expressed in *inverted* form.

Modulate from a *major* key . . .

1. to its *dominant* (V):

a. I-----I–VI⁽⁶⁾
       II⁽⁶⁾–V–I

b. I-----I
     IV–V–I

2. to its *relative minor* (VI):

    a. I-----I–II
          IV–V–I

    b. I-----I–IV
          VI–IV–V–I

3. to its *subdominant* (IV):

    a. I-----I–II
          VI–II–V–I

    b. I-----I–VI
          III–IV–V–I

4. to its *mediant* (III):

    a. I-----I–VI
          IV–V–I

    b. I-----I
          VI–♭II^6–V–I
           (Neap.)

Exercise 6·5

Modulate from a *minor* key . . .

1. to its *relative major* (III):

    a. I-----I–IV$^{(6)}$
          II$^{(6)}$–V–I

    b. I-----I
          VI–IV (or II)–V–I

2. to its *minor dominant* (V):

    a. I-----I
          IV–V–I

    b. I-----I–VI^6
          ♭II^6–V–I
          (Neap.)

3. to its *subdominant* (IV):

    a. I-----I–VI
          III–IV–V–I

    b. I-----I–IV
          I–IV–V–I

4. to its *submediant* (VI):

    a. I-----I
           III–IV (or II⁶)–V–I

    b. I-----I–IV
           VI–II⁶–V–I

5. to its *subtonic* (VII) (e.g., G minor to F major):

    a. I-----I
           II–V–I

    b. I-----I–V♭
           VI–IV–V–I

Another Approach

While the concept of the pivot chord is a time-honored one in the teaching of modulation, it can be cumbersome in both theory and practice. A somewhat different, and possibly more musical, formulation is presented herewith.

Conceive of the modulation as a progression from a given tonic triad in root position to some other root-position triad, which we call the *goal chord,* in the *same* key—for example, from I to the goal of V, or I to III. Each of these two chords—the opening one and the goal—will then be expanded (prolonged) in ways appropriate respectively to the opening and the closing of a phrase. In particular, the goal chord will receive a perfect authentic cadence in *its* key. For example, from an opening A major tonic, a modulation could occur, say, to the key of V, that is, E major, or to the key of III, that is, C♯ minor. To realize such a large-scale progression, create a predominantly stepwise soprano melody that starts on the root, third, or fifth of the tonic chord and moves (wholly diatonically for the present) to the root of the goal chord. Then harmonize this melody in four parts diatonically.

For example, let us modulate from G major to the key of its V.

Step 1

Fix the first and the last two bass tones in mind.

I   D major   V   I

Step 2

Decide on the soprano's opening note and final two notes.

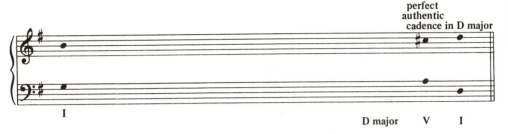

Step 3

Ascertain the meter and complete the soprano line. Let it first center upon one or more tones of the I chord, then move toward the goal. Use diatonic intervals only.

Step 4

Harmonize diatonically in four parts. (Review the point made under **Nota bene** on page 62.)

It is true, of course, that at least one chord somewhere in the middle of such a modulation can be construed as a pivot chord. But fastening on the idea of a pivot can be an awkward and mechanical procedure that impedes genuinely musical thinking. The procedure given here does not guarantee a perfect solution on the first try, but it may offer a greater chance of ultimate success than the pivot chord approach.

Exercise 6·6

Harmonize at the keyboard the following modulating melodies. When melody tones are missing, fill them in as suggested on page 67:

Major Mode   From I to V

From I to VI

From I to III

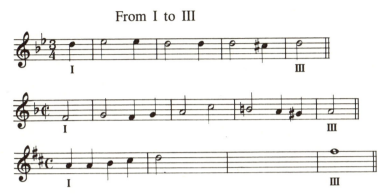

Exercise 6·7

Minor Mode

From I to III

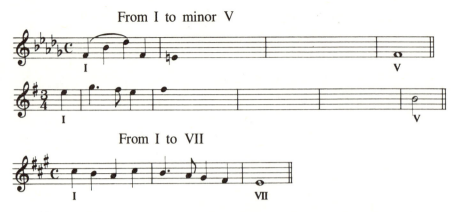

From I to minor V

From I to VII

The modulation techniques presented so far have dealt exclusively with modulation to diatonically related keys, as defined in the introduction to this chapter. The techniques presented from this point on permit modulation to chromatically related keys, without necessarily ruling out the diatonic ones.

Some of the following exercises are based on the pivot chord concept, others are not.

A Chromatic Chord Introduces the New Key
1: A Pivot Chord Exhibiting Mode Mixture

Modulation to certain chromatically related keys can be swiftly accomplished with the help of mixtures (borrowed tones, simple alterations, etc.) occurring in the pivot chord. Study the chords marked with an asterisk in the following exercise, then complete a modulation to each of the keys indicated.

Exercise 6·8

a.

Proceed to a cadence

    in E♭ major
    in A♭ major
    in D♭ major
    in B♭ minor

b.

Proceed to a cadence

    in G major
    in F major
    in A minor
    in D minor

c.

A Chromatic Chord Introduces the New Key
2: An Applied Dominant

Exercise 6·9

This opening: 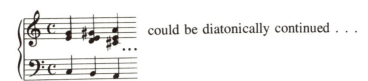 could be diatonically continued . . .

. . . in A major, thus:

. . . or in D major, thus:

. . . or in C♯ minor, thus:

. . . or in what other keys?

The crucial chord in all these examples is the second one—the V_3^4 of the A major chord—since it ushers in the new key. In similar manner lead each of the following chord sequences to cadences in keys other than D major. Take each one to several different keys.

A Chromatic Chord Introduces the New Key
3: An Augmented Sixth Chord*

Exercise 6·10

An augmented sixth chord can be a particularly effective avenue into a new key. For example:

First establish the opening key. Then move smoothly to the augmented sixth chord. Find more than one way of doing this.

Another example:

Optional: It is quite permissible to pass through other chromatic chords on the way to the augmented sixth:

Also, enharmonic change may occur in moving into the augmented sixth. In the following example the change occurs in the bass, but it may be found in any voice.

---

* We refer here only to the classical usage of the augmented sixth chord—that in which the chord's bass note lies a half step above the root of V.

Exercise 6·11

Taking the examples above as models, play the following modulations as indicated. Use all three soprano positions in the openings. The point to aim for is the bass note of the new key's augmented sixth chord. The same augmented sixth chord may lead to either a major or a minor key. Give each modulation a convincing rhythmic shape.

As a preliminary study, play only the four chords implied by the given bass notes. Then complete the exercise.

A Chromatic Chord Introduces the New Key
4: An Enharmonically Changed Diminished Seventh Chord

Any diminished seventh chord may undergo enharmonic change of one or more notes so as to become the VII[07] or an applied (secondary) VII[07] in a new key.

Exercise 6·12

Complete each modulation as indicated. A model ending is given. Begin each modulation with the given incipit in F major. In each case the enharmonically changed diminished seventh is marked with an asterisk. Try to relate the ending stylistically to the incipit by employing chromatic chords in the new key. There is no set length. Retain the meter clearly.

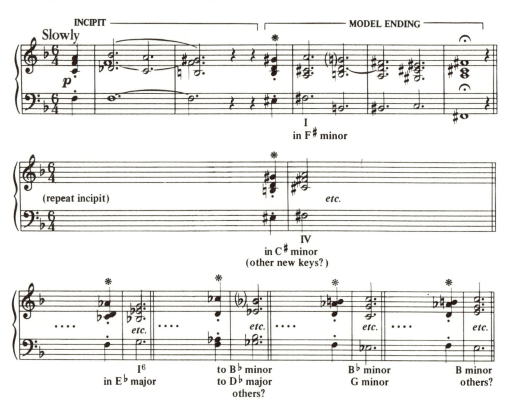

A Sequence[†] Leads to the New Key

In composition, a new key is sometimes ushered in by means of a chord sequence. The final chord in the sequence may be thought of as the first chord in the new key.

†See Chapter Five (Diatonic Sequences), *Exercise 5·4* on page 54 , and Chapter Eight, section on Chromatic Sequences, page 111.

Illustrations

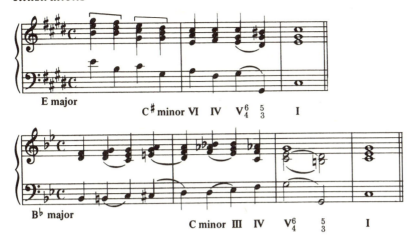

E major   C♯ minor VI IV V$_4^6$ $_3^5$ I

B♭ major   C minor III IV V$_4^6$ $_3^5$ I

Exercise 6·13

Continue the chord sequence to the last written note, then cadence in the key(s) indicated.

to B♭ minor

to F♯ minor
B minor

A minor
to E minor
B minor

F minor
to A♭ major
C minor

75

MODULATION

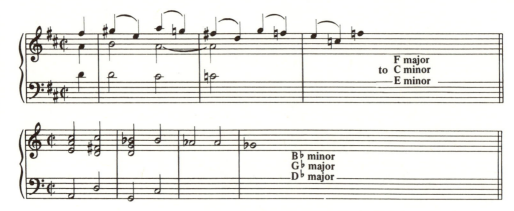

F major
to C minor
E minor

B♭ minor
G♭ major
D♭ major

Chromatic Passing Motion Leads to the New Key

The technique of chromatic passing motion presented in detail on pages 113-115 may be adapted to the purpose of modulation. As noted there, some of the exercises on those pages may be considered modulations. They should be mastered before playing those given below, which add the element of meter.

Exercise 6·14

(fill in inner voices)

CHAPTER

Seven

Figured Bass

Introduction

Figured bass or thoroughbass is a shorthand system for notating certain pitch elements of music. It consists of a bass line written in conventional notes with harmonies and some melodic elements indicated by arabic numbers (figures). These numbers denote intervals above the bass notes.

Figured bass was developed during the Baroque era and is the foundation of virtually all concerted music of that period. In this repertoire, the ensemble of instruments playing from the bass part is called the *continuo*. The size and makeup of the continuo will vary depending on the type of work, but basically it consists of 1) a keyboard instrument, and 2) one or more bass instruments. Only the keyboardist is concerned with the figures: While his left hand plays the bass line only, his right plays a realization of the figures. How to translate those figures into sound is the subject of this chapter.

The study of figured bass does more than promote understanding of Baroque music, for its principles apply to all tonal music. For this reason it has formed an important part of the musician's basic training for centuries. Practicing realization of a figured bass fosters fluent harmonic understanding and allows even those of limited keyboard ability to acquire a first-hand acquaintance with basic principles. First master thoroughly the simplest and most common figured-bass symbols, and be able to play them easily from given outer voices. For this purpose we have included a considerable number of figured-bass chorales of varying degrees of difficulty. Mastery of these will greatly simplify the next step—playing from a bass line only. It is at this point that the player becomes something of a composer, for he must supply not just inner voices, but a top line which has an interesting melodic character of its own.

From the outset, make every attempt to read and play without writing anything out. Also, remember that the figured bass system is complete in itself, and one can therefore use it without analyzing the harmonies in terms of roman numerals.

77

Basic Features

1. Arabic numbers (figures) written below (or above) a bass note denote the interval from that note to an upper voice without specifying voice, register, or doubling.

2. In general, a four-voice texture is desired, with the right hand playing three notes in close position while the left plays the bass only. Occasionally, it will be necessary or desirable to modify this arrangement by adding an extra voice to a chord, or omitting one voice, or playing in open position. For example, in the realization of a $^6_3$ chord, the right-hand part may be spread to the span of an octave (as in *a,* below) or be expressed in close position (see *b*).

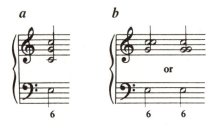

In fast instrumental music, however, consecutive sixth chords over a stepwise bass may be realized as three-voice chords, thus:

3. The figures themselves do not differentiate between chord tones and non-chord tones.

4. Key signatures operate for notes indicated by figures exactly the way they do for written notes.

5. A bass note with no figure beneath it is generally interpreted as the root of a triad. For greater certainty a triad is sometimes indicated by a ^{5}, a ^{3}, or by $^5_3$.

6. An accidental placed beside a figure means the same thing as one placed beside a written note. However, the accidental is customarily placed after the figure rather than before it (e.g., 4♯, 6♮).

7. A stroke through a figure raises the indicated note a chromatic half step. For example, $\not{5}$ or 5^+ means 5♯.

8. An accidental standing alone is an abbreviated way of altering the *third* above the bass. Thus ♯ means 3♯.

9. Further common abbreviations:

$$6 = \begin{smallmatrix}6\\3\end{smallmatrix} \qquad\qquad \begin{smallmatrix}6\\5\end{smallmatrix} = \begin{smallmatrix}6\\5\\3\end{smallmatrix} \qquad\qquad 2 \text{ or } \begin{smallmatrix}4\\2\end{smallmatrix} = \begin{smallmatrix}6\\4\\2\end{smallmatrix}$$

$$7 = \begin{smallmatrix}7\\5\\3\end{smallmatrix} \qquad\qquad \begin{smallmatrix}4\\3\end{smallmatrix} = \begin{smallmatrix}6\\4\\3\end{smallmatrix} \qquad\qquad 4 \ \ (\text{or } 4\sharp) = \begin{smallmatrix}6\\4\sharp\\2\end{smallmatrix}$$

$$5\flat = \begin{smallmatrix}5\flat\\3\end{smallmatrix}$$

10. A dash between two figures (e.g., 5–6) means that both notes should lie in the same voice. (Notational practice, however, is not consistent; hyphens are frequently left out.)

11. A line after a figure instructs the player to hold the chord struck in the right hand; thus, the note(s) lying directly over the line should not be harmonized. In this example, the bass D is a passing tone. (In many older editions, the line is not found.)

12. Figures under a rest: Where the rest is at the beginning of a beat, the implied bass note is the one *after* the rest. (See the Handel aria from *Lucrezia,* page 95 .) Where the rest occurs on a weak beat or at the end of a beat, the figures apply to the bass note *before* the rest. In that case they usually mark the resolution of a previous harmony. (See the Bach aria from *Cantata No. 21,* page 96.)

13. The term *tasto solo* (or simply *t.s.*) directs the player to play the bass line only, with no harmonies in the right hand.

Figures Involving Nonchord Tones

As implied in No. 3 above, figures are used to indicate both chord tones and nonchord tones, and do not themselves differentiate between them. It is the player who must make the determination by analyzing the specific musical context.

A very common example of a figured nonchord tone is the notation 8–7, in which the 7 is an unaccented passing tone, thus:

Likewise 6–5, thus:

6   5

Suspensions also are frequently indicated by figures. For example, the number ^{4} usually stands for $^5_4$, with the 4th as a suspension over the bass, thus:

 indicates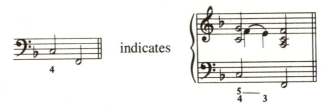

The figurings ^{7}, $^6_5$, and $^6_4_2$ can have both chordal and nonchordal interpretations, as follows:

^{7} can indicate a suspension needing resolution (*a*), as well as a functional seventh chord (*b*):

$^6_5$ can indicate a suspension resolving into a $^6_4$ chord, as well as the first inversion of a seventh chord:

$^6_4_2$ can refer to a bass suspension resolving to a root-position seventh chord, as well as the more usual third inversion of a seventh chord:

Some other examples involving nonchord tones:

the figuring $\frac{5}{4}$ may indicate a bass suspension resolving to a first-inversion seventh chord:

$\frac{7}{4}$ or $\frac{9}{7}$ can denote an accented bass passing tone, resolving perhaps to a triad in either $\frac{5}{3}$ or $\frac{6}{3}$ position:

Possible harmonies over a pedal point:

Figured Bass Exercises

Five types of composition are represented in the following exercises. They are:

Chorales, with soprano and bass given
Recitatives with figured bass
Arias with figured bass
Instrumental melodies with figured bass
Unfigured basses

In all but the first type, the figured bass and its realization constitute the accompaniment. In playing such an accompaniment, two principles must be kept in mind. First, the main voices are the solo part and the bass. The other parts are in the nature of a filler. Therefore the texture need not consist of five independent voices. At times five voices may occur, but the right-hand part may freely double the solo at any time, and parallel unisons or octaves resulting from such doublings are acceptable. Second, the accompanist must be sensitive to range and spacing. For example, if the solo is in the soprano range, the accompaniment generally should lie below the solo.

In the Baroque era, figured bass practice was so much a part of the musician's experience that sometimes composers omitted the figures altogether, assuming that everyone would understand the implications of the bass line itself. Our selection concludes with a few examples of such unfigured basses.

Chorales

Before starting on your realization, decide where the phrases begin and end.

Exercise 7·1

Heil' ger Geist, du Tröster mein

Try to determine the metrical organization of the following unbarred chorales.

Exercise 7·2

Ermuntre dich, mein schwacher Geist

Exercise 7·3

Ach Gott und Herr

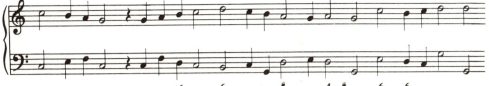

Exercise 7·4

Crüger, *Herzliebster Jesu*

Exercise 7·5

Vom Himmel hoch

Exercise 7·6

Crüger, *Nun komm, der Heiden Heiland*

Exercise 7·7

J. S. Bach, *Schaff's mit mir* from *Anna Magdalena Bach Büchlein*

Nota bene: In some of the following chorales, not all of the embellishments are indicated by figures. The player must work them out from the musical context. *Exercises 7·8, 7·9,* and *7·11,* as well as *Exercise 7·7,* can be realized more freely than the others, since they are songs rather than chorales. In these, the realization may vary in texture from three to four or even five parts, depending on the spacing allowed by the given outer voices and the exigencies of voice leading.

Exercise 7·8

J. S. Bach, *Seelen Bräutigam* from *Schemelli Gesangbuch*

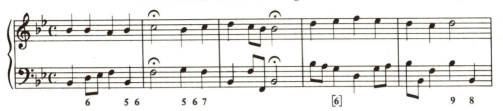

In the two places where $\begin{smallmatrix}6\\5\\b\end{smallmatrix}$ is indicated, the given doubling necessitates five-voice chords. Do the barlines accurately convey the metrical organization of this piece?

Exercise 7·9

J. S. Bach, *Gieb dich zufrieden* from *Schemelli Gesangbuch*

Exercise 7·10

J. S. Bach, *Herr Gott, dich loben alle wir*

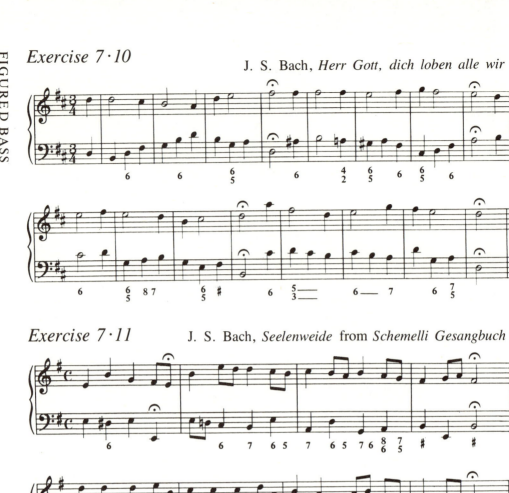

Exercise 7·11

J. S. Bach, *Seelenweide* from *Schemelli Gesangbuch*

Exercise 7·12

Antes, *Soul, at This Most Solemn Season* *

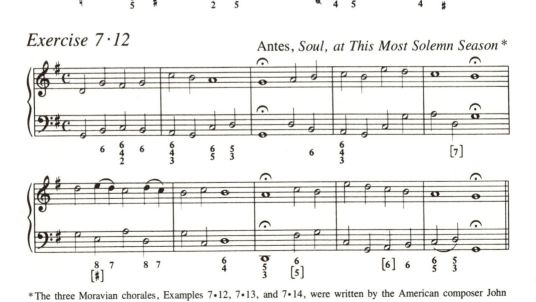

*The three Moravian chorales, Examples 7•12, 7•13, and 7•14, were written by the American composer John Antes (1740–1811).

Exercise 7·13

Antes, *Christ, the Lord, the Lord Most Glorious*

Exercise 7·14

Antes, *O Deepest Grief*

Exercise 7·15

J. S. Bach, *Wir Christenleut'* from *Christmas Oratorio*

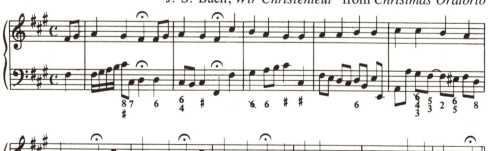

Recitatives with Figured Bass

Realizing an accompaniment to a recitative is a fairly straightforward procedure. The harmonies are clearly indicated by the figures. They show the constantly shifting key relationships characteristic of Baroque and Classical recitatives. Root-position V–I resolutions mark only the principal section cadences; others are leading-tone resolutions.

Many performance practices in the seventeenth and eighteenth centuries were not explicitly notated. Three of these are illustrated in the first Handel recitative immediately following, two affecting the melodic line, and the third, the keyboard part. 1) and 2) show the substituted appoggiaturas typical of Baroque recitative. 3) demonstrates the delay customary in the keyboard part in order to give the voice time to finish its phrase before the cadence.

2) and 3) are usually notated explicitly by Bach (see the Bach recitative in *Exercise 7·18,* m. 8), though not by Handel. 1) is generally left to the performer by both Bach and Handel.

Exercise 7·16

a.

Handel, Three Recitatives from *Messiah*

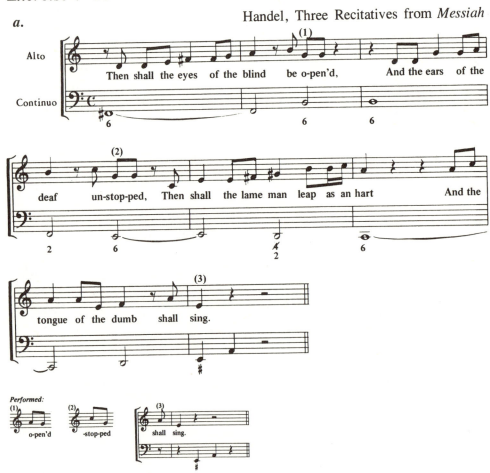

b.

Bass: Be-hold, I tell you a mys-te-ry: We shall not all sleep, but we shall all be chang'd in a mo-ment in the twink-ling of an eye, at the last trum-pet.

c.

Soprano: And the an-gel said un-to them, Fear not: for be-hold, I bring you good ti-dings of great joy which shall be to all peo-ple. For un-to you is born this day in the ci-ty of Da-vid a sa-vior, which is Christ, the Lord.

Performed:
(1) peo-ple   (3) Da-vid

2) and 4): See note 3) in the first recitative, and the explanation in the introduction to this section.

Exercise 7·17

Handel, from *Lucrezia*, Cantata for Soprano and Continuo

8): See note 3) in the first Handel recitative, and also the explanation in the introduction to this section.

trai-tor

Exercise 7·18

J. S. Bach, from *Cantata No. 170, Vergnügte Ruh', beliebte Seelenlust*

Performed:

91

Exercise 7·19

Rameau, from Cantata *L'Impatience*

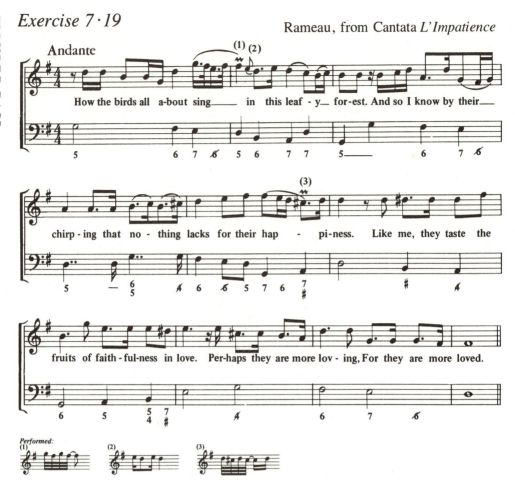

How the birds all a-bout sing___ in this leaf - y___ for-est. And so I know by their___ chirp - ing that no - thing lacks for their hap ― pi-ness. Like me, they taste the fruits of faith - ful-ness in love. Per-haps they are more lov - ing, For they are more loved.

Performed:

Songs and Arias with Figured Bass

Exercise 7·20

Telemann, *Der Frühling,* from *Odes, Book VII*

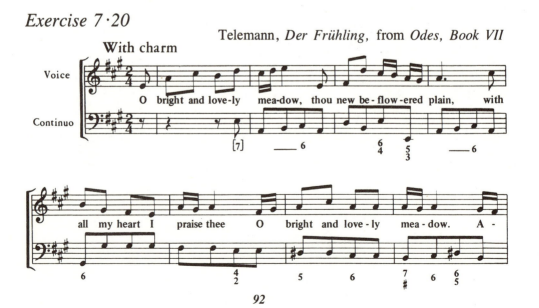

With charm

Voice

O bright and love-ly mea-dow, thou new be - flow-ered plain, with

Continuo

all my heart I praise thee O bright and love - ly mea-dow. A -

Figures in brackets [ ] are added.

(1) *Performed:*
plain

Exercise 7·21   Telemann, *Die dürstige Natur*

Voice

The earth it-self must drink   of both the rain and snow   and
The sea drinks from the air,   the sun drinks from the sea   the

Continuo

trees_up-on—their own____ sap_must like   -   wise____   nour - ish.
moon must like-wise draw_up-on_the sun____   to____   flour - ish. My

friends, since this you know,   why do   you all com-plain,   if

I a-long the way,   too,   have_ a lit - tle drink?

Exercise 7·22

Humphrey, Anthem, *O Lord My God*

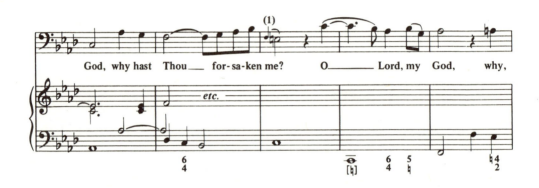

(1) *Performed:*

and art   so far___ from my health and from the words of   my   com-plaint? Why

♭   6   5   6   7   7   4   ♮3

hast Thou for-sa - ken   me and art so far___ from my health and from the words of___

6   ♮   7   6   7   6
              ♮   4   ♭

my___   com-plaint? Why   hast Thou for-sa - ken   me and art so far___ from the

6   ♮   6   ♮   7
4   5   ♮
     ♮

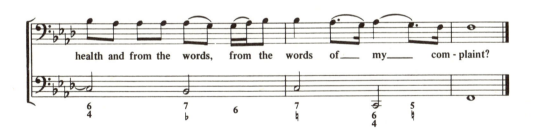

health and from the   words,   from the   words   of___   my___   com - plaint?

6   7   6   7   ⎯   5
4   ♭   ♮   6   ♮
                   4

Exercise 7·23

Handel, from Cantata *Lucrezia*

Exercise 7·24

J. S. Bach, from *Cantata No. 21, Ich hatte viel Bekümmernis*

Sigh-ing, weep-ing, sor-row, care,___ Sigh-ing,

weep-ing an-xious yearn-ing   fear and death   nag and gnaw my ach-ing

heart, tear my trou-bled soul a - part, Sigh-ing, weep-ing, sor-row, care, sor - row,

care, an-xious yearn-ing   fear and death,   Sigh - ing, weep-ing, sor - row

care, sigh-ing, weep-ing, sor-row care, nag and gnaw my ach-ing heart, tear_ my trou-bled soul a -

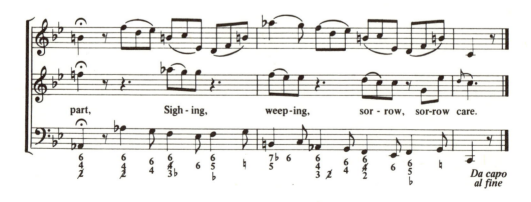

part,   Sigh - ing,   weep-ing,   sor - row,   sor-row care.

Da capo al fine

98

Solo Instrument with Figured Bass

Exercise 7·25

Corelli, Preludio from *Sonata for Violin and Continuo*,
Op. 5, No. 6

Exercise 7·26

Handel, Siciliana from *Sonata for Flute and Basso Continuo*, Op. 1, No. 11

Exercise 7·27

Handel, Bourée from *Sonata for Flute and Basso Continuo*, Op. 1, No. 5

FIGURED BASS

Flute

Continuo

Exercise 7·28

Handel, Menuetto from *Sonata for Flute and Basso Continuo,* Op. 1, No. 5

Unfigured Basses

Unfigured basses are realized in exactly the same way as their figured-bass counterparts, though the absence of figures allows you somewhat more leeway in your range of chord choices.

In the chorales, the given top line removes much of the harmonic ambiguity. Watch for accented dissonant tones in a moving bass, as well as for the structural cadences. There are many opportunities for applied dominants and for the suspensions so typical of the Baroque style.

In the unfigured recitatives, as in the earlier recitatives with figured basses, the harmonies are generally implicit in the vocal lines. Usually there is only one chord to each new note in the bass, though you will notice occasional changes of harmony within a single bass note. Study the recitatives carefully before you play them. Keep in mind the frequent key changes characteristic of recitative style, and check your harmonic choices for the logic of their resolutions as well as for their compatability with the vocal line.

In the arias, as in the recitatives, the harmonies are embedded in the vocal line. However, the bass no longer provides mere harmonic punctuation; it is more active, with much more melodic interest of its own and many embellishing and passing tones. Study the tonal organization of the piece, noting the phrase cadences and modulations which help to give it shape. Choose your chords in such a way that the harmonic structure emerges clearly through the wealth of contrapuntal detail.

Exercise 7·29   J. S. Bach, *Es kostet viel, ein Christ zu sein* from *Schemelli Gesangbuch*

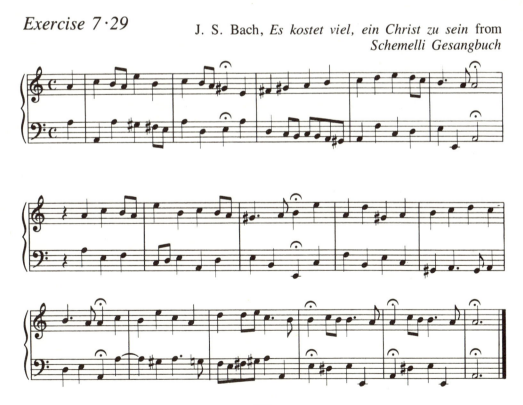

Exercise 7·30

J. S. Bach, Recitative from *Cantata No. 1, Wie schön leuchtet der Morgenstern*

Our hearts re-joice   in no false light,   nor emp - ty earth - ly

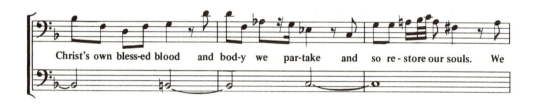

love   a light_____   of joy from God a - bove is shin - ing,   of

Christ's own bless-ed blood   and bod-y we   par-take   and   so re-store our souls.   We

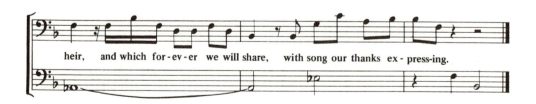

thus re-ceive His all   a-bun-dant bless - ing   to which our faith has made us

heir,   and which for-ev-er we will share,   with song our thanks ex - press-ing.

Exercise 7·31

J. S. Bach, Recitative from *Cantata No. 90, Es reisset euch ein schrecklich Ende*

Exercise 7·32

J. S. Bach, *Bist du bei mir* from *Anna Madgalena Bach*
Büchlein

If thou be near, then could I wel - come A death that_

were for me_ re - pose, my____ death, that were for me re-pose.

If thou_ be_ near, then could I wel - come A death that_

were for me re - pose, My____ death, that were for me re-pose.

Fine.

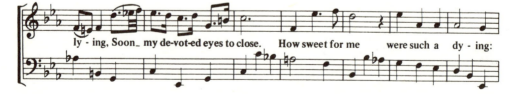

How sweet for me were such a dy - ing: Thy hand up - on my fore-head_

ly - ing, Soon_ my de-vot-ed eyes to close. How sweet for me were such a dy - ing:

Thy hand up - on my fore-head_ ly - ing, Soon_ my de-vot - ed eyes to close.

Dal segno al fine

CHAPTER

Eight

Further Exploration of Chromaticism

This chapter includes exercises in:

Applied (secondary) V and VII chords
Mode mixture (including IV$\flat$, II$_\flat^6$, flatted sixth, and Neapolitan sixth)
Augmented sixth/diminished third
Chromatic sequences
Chromatic passing motion

Applied (Secondary) V and VII Chords

The exercises below are roman numeral progressions. Play each progression, preceding each roman numeral (except the opening and closing I) with some form of an applied (secondary) V or VII chord. The applied chords may take any of the following forms:

V and V^6
V^7 and its inversions
VII^7 (as diminished or half-diminished seventh chord) and its
    inversions.

In each progression, a cadential V in root position should, whenever possible, be elaborated by the cadential $^6_4$.

Each exercise has many possible solutions. For example, here are two different solutions for the progression I–II–V$^{6-5}$–I:

I   II   V^6 ^{5} I   I   II   V^6 ^{5} I

107

Similarly, the progression I–III–IV–V–I might be realized in the following two ways:

Choose different keys for each exercise. Play several versions of each one, experimenting with a variety of soprano lines. Keep the voice leading generally quite smooth. Each solution should be in a definite rhythm. As your fluency increases, some figuration may be added (see example *c* above).

Progressions for Major Keys   *Progressions for Minor Keys*

Exercise 8·1	I–IV–V–I	*Exercise 8·9*	I–IV–V–I
Exercise 8·2	I–II–V$^{6-5}$–I	*Exercise 8·10*	I–VI–IV–V–I
Exercise 8·3	I–VI–IV–V–I	*Exercise 8·11*	I–VI–III–IV–V–I
Exercise 8·4	I–VI–IV–II–V^6–I	*Exercise 8·12*	I–III–IV–V–I
Exercise 8·5	I–VI–III–IV–V–I	*Exercise 8·13*	I–VII–VI–♭II^6–V–I
Exercise 8·6	I–V–VI–II^6–V–I	*Exercise 8·14*	I–VI^6–IV^6–♭II^6–V–I
Exercise 8·7	I–V^6–IV^6–II^6–V–I	*Exercise 8·15*	I–V^6–IV^6–III^6–♭II^6–V–I
Exercise 8·8	I–II–IV–V–VI–V–I		

Mode Mixture (Borrowed Tones, Simple Alteration)

Neapolitan ⁶₃ and ⁵₃

The Neapolitan chords are studied under the heading of mode mixture in accordance with the theory that the flatted second degree of the scale is a borrowing from the parallel Phrygian mode. Thus minor and Phrygian are mixed, as are major and Phrygian when the Neapolitan chord appears in the major mode.

Compare Chopin, *Prelude*, Op. 28, No. 20, ending.

Compare Beethoven, *Eroica Symphony*, I, mm. 272–83.

Other Uses of Mixture

Play the following progressions in various keys. Notice that for the opening and closing chords of each progression the soprano position has been indicated with a carat (ˆ): thus, $\hat{\underset{I}{3}}$ means "tonic chord with third scale degree in the soprano."

As a model, here is the solution to *Exercise 8·30* as it would appear in E major:

$$\underset{I}{\hat{8}} \quad \flat III \quad IV^\flat \quad \underset{I}{\hat{5}}$$

Notice that accidentals have been notated throughout by means of ♭ and ♮ only. The ♭ requires the player to *lower* and the ♯ to *raise* the indicated note a chromatic half step. When the ♭ appears to the left of the roman numeral, as in ♭III above, the root of the chord is flattened, that is, lowered by a half step from its diatonic position.

Play in Major Keys

Exercise 8·24 $\underset{I}{\hat{3}}-IV-II\,^7_{\flat 5}-V^7-\underset{I}{\hat{3}}$

Exercise 8·25 $\underset{I}{\hat{8}}-IV-\flat VI^{\flat 5}-\underset{I}{\hat{8}}$

Exercise 8·26 $\underset{I}{\hat{5}}-IV^\flat-V^{\flat 9-8}_{7}-\underset{I}{\hat{5}}$

Exercise 8·27 $\underset{I}{\hat{5}}-\flat VI^{\flat 5}-II^6_{\flat 5}-V^{8-7}-\underset{I}{\hat{3}}$

Exercise 8·28 $\underset{I}{\hat{3}}-\flat VI^{\flat 5}-II^7_\sharp-V^7-\underset{I}{\hat{1}}$

Exercise 8·29 $\underset{I}{\hat{5}}-VII^{\flat 7}-\underset{I}{\hat{5}}$

Exercise 8·30 $\underset{I}{\hat{8}}-\flat III^{\flat 5}-IV^\flat-\underset{I}{\hat{5}}$

Exercise 8·31 $\underset{I}{\hat{5}}-\flat III^{\flat 5}-\flat VI^{\flat 5}-II^6_{\flat 5}-V^{\flat 9}_7-\underset{I}{\hat{5}}$

Exercise 8·32 $\underset{I}{\hat{8}}-III^\sharp-V-\underset{I}{\hat{8}}$

Play in Minor Keys

Exercise 8·33   I–IV$^\sharp$–I

Exercise 8·34   I–III$^\flat$–IV$^\sharp$– $\flat$II–V$^\sharp$–I

Exercise 8·35   I–$\sharp$III$^\sharp$–V$^\flat$–III–IV$^\sharp$–VI–I$^\sharp$

Augmented Sixth/Diminished Third

Experiment with realizations of the two unfigured basses in *Exercises 8·36* and *8·37* as follows:

At ① use:

    a. augmented $\frac{6}{3}$ ("Italian sixth")

    b. augmented $\frac{6}{4}{}_{3}$ ("French sixth")

    c. augmented $\frac{6}{5}{}_{3}$ ("German sixth")

At ② use inversions of the chords listed under ①. Memorize the realization you like best—and play it in other keys.

Exercise 8·36

Exercise 8·37

111

Chromatic Sequences

Chromatic sequences can occur either in passages that are basically in one key, or in modulations. The five exercises below are of the former type. The brackets indicate where sequences are to occur. Complete the exercises at the keyboard, then transpose them to other keys.*

Exercise 8·38

Exercise 8·39

Exercise 8·40

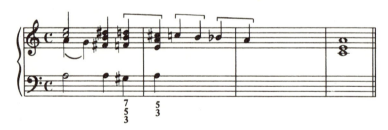

Exercise 8·41

*Exercises in sequences (both diatonic and chromatic) that occur in *modulatory* passages will be found on pages 74-76.

Exercises 8·42   Adapted from Schubert, *String Quintet,* Op. 163, III

Chromatic Passing Motion

Each of the following exercises is based on a given framework consisting of two chords which are to be understood as the beginning and end of a progression. The length of the progression is determined by the player. Realize the progression by playing a series of chords that moves smoothly, that is, "passes," from the first given chord to the last. There are many good solutions for each framework. Play each exercise a number of times, making each version different.

Procedure:

> The bass and one of the three upper voices, usually the soprano, move most often in contrary motion; they will either move exclusively in half steps or one voice will retain a single note.
> The remaining two voices are not restricted to motion in half steps. They move as smoothly as possible.
> The individual chords in the series may consist of any triad, seventh chord, or augmented sixth chord in any inversion.

Study the following illustration, which shows three ways of completing one framework. In all three, the voice that moves contrary to the bass is the soprano. You will observe tied notes in the outer voices. Why must some notes be repeated from one chord to another?

Illustrations

Given framework

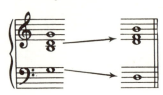

Solution a

Solution b

Solution c

In like manner, fill in the following frameworks, keeping the goal chord firmly in mind as you proceed. Test every solution with your ear!

Exercises 8·43   8·44   8·45   8·46

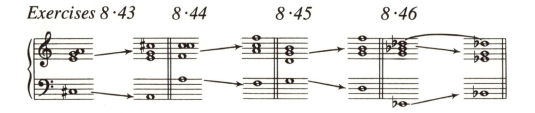

Exercises 8·47   8·48*   8·49

Exercises 8·50   8·51

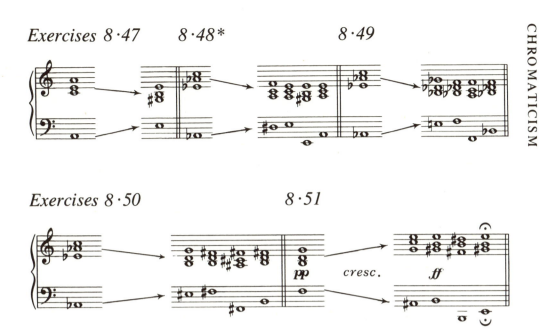

pp   cresc.   ff

* From *Exercises 8·48* on, cadences are added at the end of each framework. In these cases, the passing motion may be conceived as effecting a modulation from one key to another. (See also page 76.)

Nine

Improvisation

Improvisation is the act of inventing music as you play it. Although such a performance may result in the creation of something new, it more often consists of elaboration of music already composed, as in jazz or the ornamentation of a Baroque melody. Both practices have played significant roles in the history of music.

Quite aside from these considerations, however, improvisation can also contribute much to the development of a music student's skill and understanding. First, events move quickly in improvisation; you must respond quickly and you hear the results of your effort immediately. Second, you are encouraged to be inventive, to think of many different ways of solving each problem. And improvisation can yield many musical satisfactions, too. An imaginative improvisation is worthy of a listener's attention just as surely as if it had been a composition committed to paper after many hours of careful consideration.

In executing the exercises below, bear one caution in mind: do not let the fingers fall aimlessly on the keys. First think, then play; continue to think while playing. What you are attempting is not piano playing but rather thinking at the keyboard. Avoid continuous arpeggiation, which may sound pleasant for a moment but holds up the musical motion. Be aware of soprano and bass lines and what their goals are.

Always have a specific rhythm in mind: determine the meter and tempo in advance. A series of even note values is not very interesting; vary the durations as much as seems desirable. Use different keys and modes.

This chapter includes five types of exercises:

Improvising Melodies
Improvising phrases in four-part harmony
Elaborating chord progressions
Improvising variations on a given theme
Improvising periods using motivic elaboration

Improvising Melodies

Exercise 9·1: Improvising Short Phrases

Improvise two- or four-measure phrases in 2/4, 3/4, 4/4, 6/8, and ₵ time so that each begins and ends on a tone of the tonic triad, that is, the first, third, or fifth degrees of the scale. To discourage wandering, insure the coherence of the melody by establishing a clear sense of key. Not least of all, encourage the active participation of the imagination by limiting the number of tones to two, three, four, or, at most, five from the same key. Sections 1 through 8 in the illustrations below show what can be done within these limits. Note how each of sections 1 through 3 uses a different group of four tones from the key of G. Section 8 uses only two.

Illustrations

In addition to providing each improvised phrase with a distinctive rhythmic profile and clear sense of key and meter, try even at these early stages to be attentive to the ways in which dynamics and articulation contribute to the unique character of each improvisation.

As soon as you have performed a short phrase, can you repeat it exactly as you had originally intended to play it? While in actual practice it is unlikely that an improviser will want to repeat verbatim anything that he has already played, to be able to repeat a short phrase can demonstrate that your improvisation was indeed the result of conscious decision and not mere chance. Consider also using such improvised phrases as the basis for an ear-training exercise in which other students must repeat your phrases exactly as you have played them. If they have difficulty apprehending your improvisations, is it perhaps because certain aspects such as the rhythm were ambiguous?

Exercise 9·2:   Building Two-Phrase Units

On closer examination it can be seen that, because they do not come to rest on the key note G and therefore seem to invite at least one more phrase of equal length which will end more conclusively, several of the examples above lend themselves to further expansion into two-phrase periods of four or eight measures. With each of these phrases, as well as others of your own improvisation, now functioning as an antecedent ending in a semicadence, improvise an additional phrase of equal length to serve as a consequent phrase ending in a full cadence on the tonal center of the key. To avoid having to make too many new decisions at one time and to help insure that the consequent phrase will sound like a logical outgrowth of the antecedent phrase and be symmetrically balanced with it, use the same rhythm in both phrases.

Illustration

This illustration is based on section 3 of the illustration on page 116. Observe how the melodic shape of the consequent phrase, along with that of the antecedent phrase, contributes to the shape of the entire eight-measure period. In this example the peak of the shape occurs at the very beginning; the direction of the remainder of the melody, particularly of the second half, is a descent to the tonal center in the last measure.

Exercise 9·3:   Building Three-Phrase Units

Because it ends on the tonal center, section 4 of the illustration on page 116 suggests either a goal already reached or expansion beyond the scope of a four- or eight-measure period. The need for another phrase to return to G must be created first by improvising an intervening phrase which departs from G and ends with a semicadence. One possible solution is shown below. You can model several similar improvisations of your own after it.

Illustration

Observe how, because the first phrase lies low, the intervening phrase begins in a higher register, thus supplying the entire melody with a focal point. This phrase also ends, as so many semicadences do, on a tone a step above the tonal center. The last phrase completes the movement from this tone to the tonal center while restating the first phrase with small yet significant modifications. The result is a miniature piece in ternary form.

Exercise 9·4:   Building Four-Phrase Units

Still further expansion into double periods in binary form are possible using the same kind of melodic fragment illustrated in sections 1 through 8 of the illustration on page 116. The illustration below may be used as a model for several improvisations of your own. In it, tension is built during the first two phrases by an ascent through the tones of the tonic triad. The second half of the piece (mm. 5–8) releases this tension by descending from the high point to the tonal center in the final cadence.

Illustration

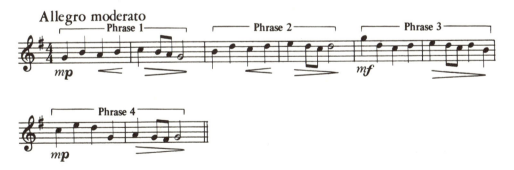

Again, in order not to introduce too many new elements at once into these increasingly difficult improvisations, retain the rhythm of phrase 1 in all the succeeding phrases with one important exception: To prevent the brief pause that occurs at the end of each of the first two phrases from becoming predictable by the end of measure 6 and from slowing the rhythmic momentum of the piece, the continuity of the rhythm from measure 6 into measure 7 is maintained by replacing the half note that would otherwise occur with two quarter notes.

As your improvisations become longer, the means needed to extend their length must necessarily become more varied and sophisticated. You will have to depend increasingly on your close study both of the improvisations of those more experienced than you and of the standard literature in order to acquire an understanding of such techniques. Note already in the illustration above how a sequence is used to create movement between the first two phrases. Can you describe the differences between the various ways in which the opening motive is used in measures 3, 5, and 7?

Although all of the exercises just described should be played on keyboard instruments, students who play other instruments should attempt these exercises on them as well.

Further practice in ear training will be possible if your instructor or a fellow student supplies an initial phrase which you must then repeat before improvising one or more additional phrases.

Improvising Phrases in Four-Part Harmony

Exercise 9·5

As you become familiar with the basic four-part harmonic progressions set forth in Chapter Two, try to employ them as early as possible in the improvisation of simple two- or four-measure phrases. As in the performance of all basic progressions, the left hand should play only the bass line while the right hand combines the upper three parts. Now more than ever it is necessary to devise a treble melody that moves predominantly by step, because a soprano that moves by many leaps will force the right hand to change position constantly and so lose control of the keys. Since they are apt to result in static melodies, avoid repeated tones unless they are prompted by the accompaniment of progressions like I–VI, where such features as a moving bass and a marked change in the quality of the chords will maintain interest.

At first, use only primary triads in these phrases. However, even when you introduce greater harmonic variety into your improvisations, these triads must retain their principal roles as key builders. Sections *a* and *b* below illustrate what can be accomplished at this early stage; sections *aa* and *bb* how the same simple treble lines can be treated in a harmonically more elaborate fashion.

While always striving to think of both melody and harmony together, indeed as different dimensions of the same musical phenomenon, it may be necessary at first to give primary consideration to the formation of a soprano line having clear direction, a line whose role is then further clarified and supported by the accompanying parts. To express this observation more simply, if less accurately, "Any good tune can be harmonized, so begin at least with a good tune!" Above all, do not play a series of chords in which the highest tones create a line by mere chance. A musical phrase can

Illustrations

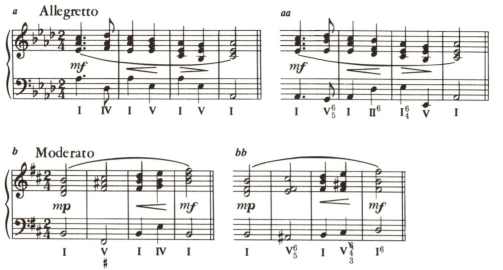

captivate only to the extent that its principal elements—melody, harmony, and rhythm—exhibit distinctive profiles.

Exercise 9·6

As you acquire greater facility, introduce occasional accessory tones such as passing and neighbor tones or suspensions. Conclude some phrases with a semicadence on the dominant, as shown in sections *c* and *d* below.

Illustrations

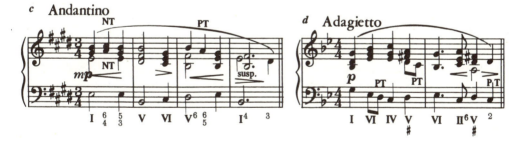

Having satisfactorily improvised several phrases ending with a semicadence on the dominant, add a consequent phrase of identical length ending with a full cadence on the tonic. A review of the principles set forth in *Exercise 9·2* concerning the improvisation of four- or eight-measure periods is useful at this point. The frequent review of such basic progressions as cadence formulae or those involving chords in second inversion is always valuable. The following illustrations show how the preceding illustrations (*c* and *d*) can be expanded to twice their length. Note in both cases how the second phrase supplies a high point from which there is the inevitable descent to the final cadence.

Illustrations

cc Andantino

dd Adagietto

The examples on page 120 provide excellent opportunities to improvise phrases of still greater length because they already end on the tonic. Before attempting them, however, review the principles set forth in the paragraph preceding those examples.

Once again the improvisation of four- or eight-measure periods can be of inestimable value in the development of aural perception if the instructor or a fellow student improvises the antecedent phrase, requiring you to repeat it verbatim before you proceed to a consequent phrase.

As you try to introduce a greater degree of chromaticism into your harmonic vocabulary, all the other elements of your improvisations, such as melody and rhythm, should remain as simple as possible. Do not depart yet from the practice of playing the three upper voices with the right hand and the bass with the left.

Notice in the following illustrations how the introduction of secondary leading-tone chromaticism tends to assign a more prominent role to the inner parts and how, partly to compensate for this new emphasis, the outer parts move almost exclusively by step. More than ever you will need to concentrate on the conduct of the outer parts of the texture, the soprano and bass lines; in practical terms the outer parts can be translated as the left hand and the higher fingers of the right hand.

Illustrations

e Con moto

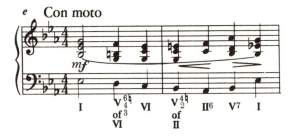

f **Allegro moderato**

Improvise phrases such as the following, which also take advantage of modal interchange (mixture). Remember that the major mode, which lacks the variety of the minor mode, usually borrows from the minor.

Illustration

g **Allegro vivo**

Elaborating Chord Progressions

Exercise 9·7

Memorize the series of chords given below. Then elaborate those chords according to the suggestions that follow. When the possibilities suggested by these examples have been exhausted, devise other beginnings, using, for instance, suspensions or appoggiature. Play these exercises in several major and minor keys.

Given chord progression

a. Elaboration by simple arpeggiation

b. Elaboration by the use of neighbor tones

c. Elaboration by the use of passing tones

d. Elaboration of the bass

Exercise 9·8

In a chaconne which probably reflected the improvisatory practice of his time, Handel composed sixty-two variations on the following ground bass:

Below are the incipits of eleven of Handel's variations. Three others which are adaptions of Handel's are also included.

Complete each variation begun in the manner of the incipit. In the course of each variation it is permissible, and occasionally even desirable, to vary the figures of the ground bass. For example:

or

You may also include in your improvisation one or more variations based on the following incipits in the minor mode:

Invent additional incipts for other variations in 2/4, 4/4, or 6/8 time, and improvise variations.

Improvising Variations on a Given Theme

Exercise 9·9

Improvising variations on a given theme is a time-honored practice, going back at least as long as there have been keyboard players. Many variations are simply embellishments of the melody and, to a lesser extent, the bass line. More complex variations elaborate the tonal structure by developing new embellishing chords.

The theme below is simple both in melody and tonal structure. Memorize it before starting to play improvisations. Each variation you improvise should be based on at least one specific technique of elaboration. As models, four beginnings are given, together with indications of the main elaborative procedure.

Dussek, *Sonata,* Op. 39, No. 1, II, Theme

a. Expansion of chords in musical space by means of arpeggiation

b. Diatonic passing tones between the notes of the chord in the right hand

c. Bass elaborated with diatonic neighbor and passing tones

d. Chromatic neighbor and passing tones

Improvising Periods Using Motivic Elaboration

The periods you will improvise in this section are considerably more ambitious than those with which you began in the first section of this chapter. They utilize all of the skills you have acquired thus far, and may be regarded as brief yet complete compositions.

Exercise 9·10

Beginning with one of the following motives,

improvise an eight-measure period whose first phrase ends with a semicadence, the second with a full cadence. The diagram below may serve as a guide. The right hand plays only the melody, the left hand the chordal accompaniment. Generally, there should be no more than one chord change for each measure. Maintain the same accompaniment pattern at least until the end of the first four measures. Before attempting to play with both hands together, it would be wise to play the left hand alone. To help prevent the melody from wandering, restrict the number of different pitches in each measure to two, three, or, at most, four. Within this plan, where would you expect the climax of the melody to occur?

Plan I

Measure	1	2	3	4
Right Hand	a motive	the same motive treated more or less sequentially but with the rhythm retained, at least	something different that will lead to a semicadence	semicadence
Left Hand	I	I	I^6, $IV^{(6)}$, or II^6	$V^{(7)}$

Measure	5	6	7	8
Right Hand	the motive exactly as played in the first measure	the motive treated again more or less sequentially but not in the same way as in measure 2	something different that will lead to measure 8	first degree of the scale, possibly the third, more rarely the fifth
Left Hand	I	II^6 or $IV^{(6)}$	I^6_4 $V^{(7)}$	I

Another possible chord plan:

Plan II

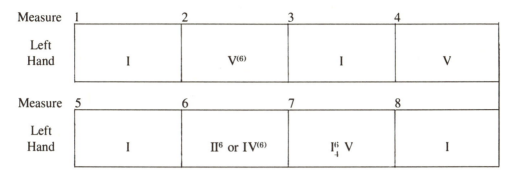

Measure	1	2	3	4
Left Hand	I	$V^{(6)}$	I	V

Measure	5	6	7	8
Left Hand	I	II^6 or $IV^{(6)}$	I^6_4 V	I

Below are two illustrations of what might be done.

Illustration for Plan I

Illustration for Plan II

Exercise 9·11:   Plan for a Double Period

Beginning with the four-measure phrase

improvise a sixteen-measure double period, using the following diagram as a guide for measures 5–16:

Right Hand	something different			
Left Hand	V^2	I^6	II^6	V

5   6   7   8

variation of measures 1–4		similar to 5–8			
as before		?	?	I^6_4 V	I

9–12

13   14   15   16

The chapter you have just completed does not pretend to convey everything that can be learned about improvisation. The possibilities are virtually limitless—as they are in any art requiring skill and invention. Rather, these exercises should be regarded as a primer with all the limitations, helpmates, and prohibitions that must be assumed by a novice embarking on a rigorous training program. The apparent strictures can be lifted without danger either to you or your listeners as you progress through persistent study and exercise.

Ten

Score Reading

Most musicians work with scores as part of their regular professional activity. The best way to learn what is in a score is to play it at the piano. Conductors and composers often have the ability to read orchestral scores at the piano without preparation. Other musicians may not develop the skill to such an advanced level, but all must be able to find out the content of the page with reasonable efficiency. The exercises in this chapter introduce the main topics of score reading in progressive order and may be prepared in advance or read at sight. They have been chosen so as to present the minimum of purely pianistic problems, although it is undeniable that for advanced playing from scores considerable pianistic proficiency is needed.

The following suggestions are offered for those with little previous experience in reading scores. Whenever possible, play the higher parts with the right hand and the bass line only with the left. *Exercise 10·3,* for example, can be played almost throughout this way:

Chords scored for large ensembles frequently employ many doublings at the octave and exceed the span of the pianist's hands. To be playable, these chords may be condensed by omitting some or all of the doublings. All the essential elements except the bass are usually playable by the right hand in close position. In condensing chords inner parts may be transposed to the register in which the right hand finds itself. Where possible, the higher and lowest parts should be played in the same registers in which they appear in the score. Thus the opening chords of *Exercise 10·9* can be played:

It is often necessary to distinguish between the principal tones and those which simply reinforce them. Because the strings outweigh the winds in the last measure of *Exercise 10·17*, the chords should be played as follows:

When the right hand is occupied completely with a line, usually of a melodic character, the inner parts must be assigned to the left hand and transposed as needed. Measures 8 and 9 of *Exercise 10·14* should be played as follows:

When dealing with a score of two or more staffs, it is necessary to read all staffs simultaneously rather than one after the other. You can train yourself to see the highest and lowest staffs at the same time by first playing only the notes on those staffs. Keep your eyes on the page; do not look at your hands unless absolutely necessary. Having another person cover your hands with a sheet of paper while you are playing will help you focus your attention on the score and not the keys.

If you have no previous experience in score reading, start with the choral excerpts in Chapter Three. They are *Exercises 3·8, 3·9, 3·10, 3·26,* and *3·37.*

Exercise 10·1: The Alto Clef (Viola Clef)

Berlioz, *Fantastic Symphony,* I

Exercise 10·2:   Alto and Bass Clefs

Beethoven, *Symphony No. 7*, II

Exercise 10·3: String Quartet

Schubert, *Death and the Maiden Quartet;* II

Exercise 10·4: Strings of the Classic Orchestra

Beethoven, *Piano Concerto No. 5,* II

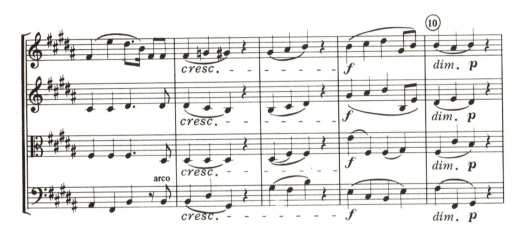

Exercise 10·5: Five-Part String Ensemble

J. S. Bach, Sinfonia from *Cantata No. 4, Christ lag in Todesbanden*

Violino I
Violino II
Viola I
Viola II
Continuo

Vl.
Vla.
Cont.

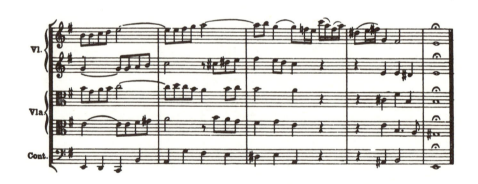

Vl.
Vla.
Cont.

136

Exercise 10·6: Winds without Transposition

Stravinsky, *Symphony of Psalms,* II

138

Exercise 10·7: Winds and Strings without Transposition

Mendelssohn, *Italian Symphony*, II

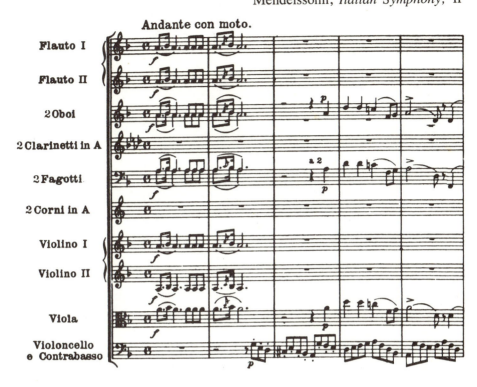

sempre staccato e p

Exercise 10·8:   Clarinet in B♭

Mozart, *Symphony No. 39*, II, Trio

Exercise 10·9:   With and without Transposition

Mozart, *Divertimento*, K. 229, II, Trio

Exercise 10·10: Strings and Winds

Copland, *Appalachian Spring*

143

Exercise 10·11: Clarinets in A and Bassoons

Tchaikovsky, *Romeo and Juliet*

Exercise 10·12: Horn in F

Britten, Prologue to *Serenade*

Exercise 10·13: Brass with Various Transpositions; English Horn

Dvořák, *Symphony From the New World,* II

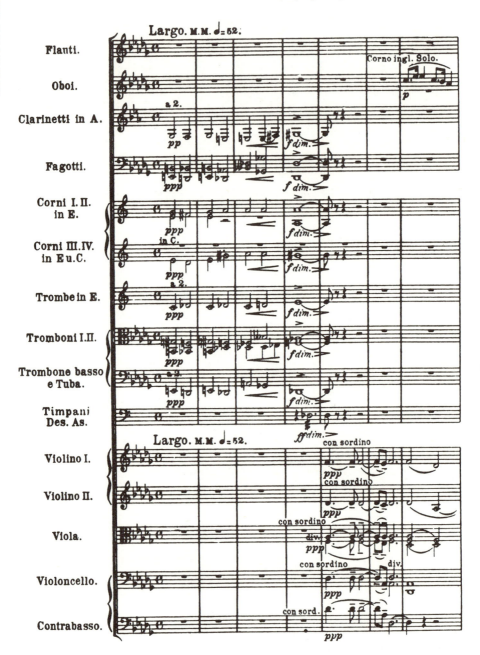

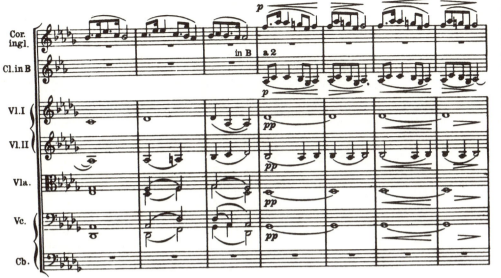

SCORE READING

Exercise 10·14:   Winds with Transposition; Strings

Tchaikovsky, *Symphony No. 5*, II

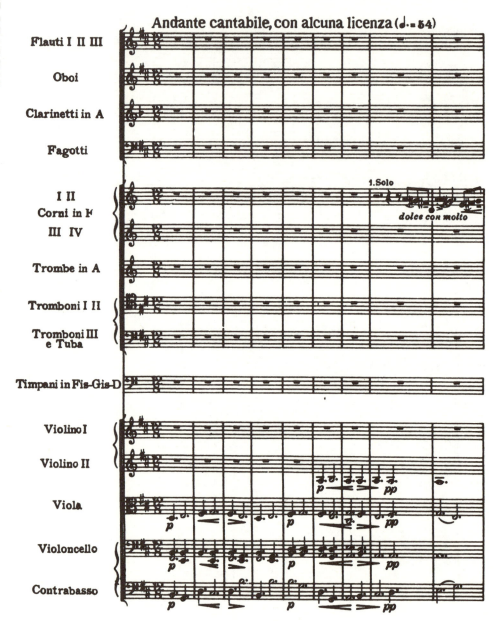

148

149

Exercise 10·15:   Tenor Clef

Stravinsky, Introduction to *The Rite of Spring* (Bassoon Part Only)

Exercise 10·16:   Tenor Clef, B♭ Clarinet, Strings

Brahms, *Symphony No. 3*, III

Exercise 10·17: The Classical Orchestra

Haydn, *Symphony No. 100,* Introduction

153

Exercise 10·18: The Romantic Orchestra

Brahms, *Symphony No. 4*, I

156

157

Exercise 10·19: The Impressionist Orchestra

Debussy, *Prelude to "The Afternoon of a Faun"*

J. S. Bach, Six Chorales in Four Clefs

Exercise 10·20

Lob und Preis sei Gott dem Va - ter und dem Sohn und dem hei-li-gen

Gei - ste, wie es war im An-fang jetzt und im - mer - dar und von

E - wig-keit zu E - wig-keit, A - men.

163

Exercise 10·21

Er - tödt' uns durch dein' Gü - te, er - weck' uns durch dein' Gnad';
den al - ten Men-schen krän - ke, dass der neu' le - ben mag wohl

hier auf die-ser Er - den, den Sinn und all' Be-gehr - den und G'dan-ken hab'n zu dir.

Exercise 10·22

Das hat er Al-les uns ge-than, sein gross' Lieb' zu zei-gen an; dess freu' sich al - le

164

Exercise 10·23

Exercise 10·24

Exercise 10·25

Soll ich denn auch des To - des Weg und fin-st're Stra - sse rei - sen,
wohl an! ich tret' auf Bahn und Steg, den mir dein' Au - gen wei-sen. Du

bist mein Hirt, der Al - les wird zu sol-chem En - de keh - ren, dass

ich ein-mal in dei-nem Saal dich e - wig mö - ge eh - ren!

CHAPTER
Eleven

A Short Keyboard Anthology

Introduction

This chapter consists of seventeen pieces which can be played by students with limited pianistic ability. The works have been chosen for practice and transposition. They represent a variety of keyboard styles, ranging from the seventeenth century to the middle of the twentieth.

You will get best results from these pieces if you memorize each one before transposing. Then correct any errors by ear, rather than by referring to the printed page. Both memorization and transposition are facilitated by analysis of a work. Begin transposition by playing the piece in closely related keys, then move to more distant ones.

Contents

1. Bartók, *Imitation and Inversion*, No. 23 from *Mikrokosmos*, Book I

2. Handel, Gavotte from *Suite in G*

3. Giles Farnaby, *A Toye* from *Fitzwilliam Virginal Book*

4. Leo Kraft, *Slow Waltz*

5. Handel, Sarabande from *Suite in D Minor*

6. Schumann, Melody from *Album for the Young*, Op. 68, No. 1

7. Mozart, *Minuet*, K. 2

8. Bartók, Ballad from *For Children*

(52")

attacca
(*ad lib.*)

9. Chopin, *Prelude*, Op. 28, No. 20

10. Allen Brings, *Imitation*

11. Schubert, *Waltz,* Op. 9, No. 16

12. Chopin, *Prelude,* Op. 28, No. 7

13. Stravinsky, Larghetto from *For the Five Fingers*

14. J. S. Bach, Sarabande from *French Suite in D Minor*

15. Prokofiev, *The Rain and the Rainbow* from *Children's Pieces*, Op. 65

16. Mozart, *Sonata in A Major,* K. 331, I, Theme

17. Beethoven, *Sonata in A♭*, Op. 26, I, Theme

Fingerings for Major and Harmonic Minor Scales in One Octave

In piano fingering, the thumb of each hand is called 1 and the other fingers are called 2, 3, 4, and 5. The fingerings for all major and harmonic minor scales in one octave are given below. Fingerings for the right hand (R.H.) are shown above the notes and the fingerings for the left hand (L.H.) are shown below the notes. The major scales are shown only in an upward direction. For downward major scales, simply read the notes and fingering from right to left. The fingering for C major is particularly important since it is also used—in both hands—for G, D, A, and E major and A, E, D, G, and C melodic minor. Scales should be practiced slowly and evenly. For each scale, play the right hand alone, then the left hand alone, and finally both hands together an octave apart.

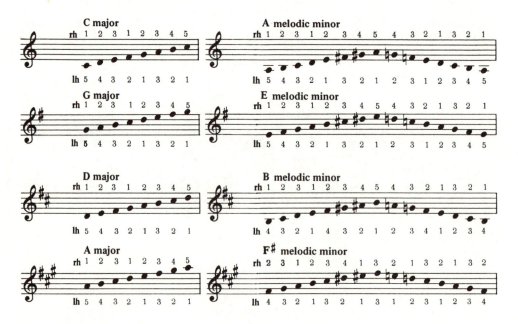